Removing
The Face

Removing The Face

*A Remedy for Pain &
Prescription for Change*

IFEDAYO GREENWAY

& 12 Courageous Women
Transformed Through Truth

REMOVING THE FACE
Published by Purposely Created Publishing Group™
Copyright © 2019 Ifedayo Greenway

All rights reserved.

No part of this book may be reproduced, distributed or transmitted in any form by any means, graphic, electronic, or mechanical, including photocopy, recording, taping, or by any information storage or retrieval system, without permission in writing from the publisher, except in the case of reprints in the context of reviews, quotes, or references.

Unless otherwise indicated, scripture quotations are from the Holy Bible, King James Version. All rights reserved.

Printed in the United States of America

ISBN: 978-1-64484-136-5

Special discounts are available on bulk quantity purchases by book clubs, associations and special interest groups. For details email: sales@publishyourgift.com or call (888) 949-6228.
For information log on to: www.PublishYourGift.com

This book is dedicated to the Movement of Becoming (MOB). It's dedicated to every one of you who has embarked on your change journey and embraced the process required to facilitate a productive and progressive life! Movement is and will always be a mandate. #MOBChics

TABLE OF CONTENTS

Foreword 1

What's in a Name, What's in a Face 5
Ifedayo Greenway

There Is Purpose in the Pit 15
Shakita Wilson

A Look Through the Looking Glass 25
Kiara Washington

This Is Not Your Assignment 35
Lynnetta M. Seabury

I Didn't Know My Own Strength 45
Sandra L. Parker

My Padded Walls 55
Felicia Ellis

Hurts, Habits, Hang-Ups, and Emotional Heredity 65
Charleta D. M. Harvey, MAML

Growing Through the Challenges of
"I'll Be Happy When . . ." 75
Laura C. Bembry

Removing the Face of the Unbearable 87
Jackie Togun

The Public Figure's Mask, Exit Stage Left 95
Monique A. J. Smith

The Journey to Becoming 105
Tabatha L. Dandridge

Finding My Voice 115
Sabrina Thomas

The Truth of the Matter Is 123
Gwendolyn Winston-Marrow

Now What? 133

About the Authors 135

FOREWORD

When Ifedayo Greenway asked me to write the foreword for *Removing the Face: A Remedy for Pain and Manuscript for Change*, I felt mixed emotions. I felt grateful for an opportunity to share, but ashamed when I reflected on what it would mean to authentically express my contribution to this subject matter. I was surprised at her invitation to work together again, because for a while now she has worked really hard to distance herself from me, mainly because of how my purpose unfolded in her life. I soon came to learn that the request for me to write this was like no other. It breaks all the rules, shattering the norm of how a typical foreword is to be written. Her request alone was symbolic of a level of forgiveness that I never expected. My agreeing to write meant that I would have to stand in my truth and acknowledge that it was forgiveness that I needed from her, and from you as well.

Up until now, I have never been held accountable, never unveiled the face that contributed to your story. Accepting this assignment meant that it was time to pull back the curtain for transparency, to right the wrong, since I have been a fountain of hurt for so many. You see, I am the face of the ones who have damaged so many lives. I can't fully explain to you how or even why I've chosen this path. I am your father, your mother, your sister, your brother, your auntie, or your uncle. I could be your ex-husband or boyfriend, your bestie or girlfriend. The fact is, when you trusted and needed me the most, my inclination was to control, belittle, misuse, abuse, reject, and disappoint. *Removing the Face* is a treasury of help toward liberation for you, the one bearing the burden of hurt and harm by the very people entrusted to love you. My hope is that it will also be a catalyst toward change for individuals like me, who negligently overstep the boundaries of others.

In the past, I've been the opportunist to whom you relinquished this influence. I, at times, have been the one to exploit trust, the one with tendencies to lie and cheat if I thought it would get me what I wanted—that was my mission from beginning to end. I pushed a false narrative of who I really was so that I would maintain complete control of our relationship. Most who have encountered me have experienced some sort of wound or grief. I failed you, and for that I take responsibility and hope that you will hear my heart when I say I'm sorry. As you navigate through the experiences of the writers within *Removing the Face*, take the time to reconsider who you allow in your space, what you invite into your atmosphere, and why. I humbly write this in hopes that it will help you discern the quality of your past, present, and future relationships, never again to fall victim to another like me.

I hope that you are aware that hurting people hurt people. Although my contribution to this book may not allow complete absolution for me, I know that it is time to embark on my own personal journey of healing. Therefore, I encourage you to choose to move beyond your pain and embrace the healing that comes with making right choices for your future. This ingenious, timely piece will impact many lives and will help you embrace all that is good and meant for you. I salute Ifedayo Greenway and each individual writer for the courage and strength to speak to the things that have held them, and you, back for so long.

Signed,
Silent Contributor to Your Pain

What's in a Name, What's in a Face

Ifedayo Greenway

Dayo is what I have been affectionately called all of my life, but my name, the one that my parents decided would be the best fit for the first offspring of their marriage and their intimate moments together, is Ifedayo. Growing up, I didn't necessarily like my name. I didn't like the fact that it wasn't "normal" and that it was so easily mispronounced. The first days of school were the worst. I always knew when the teachers had reached my name during the roll call because they would sit and stare, pondering on whether or not they would even take a stab at it. I would just raise my hand and say "here" to save them from the effort. Going to the doctor's office was no different; the nurse would come out, look at the chart, and then look around the waiting room to see if she could identify who the name belonged to. The minute we made eye contact, I would know it was my turn to be seen.

Having an uncommon name made me feel *different*, but eventually I learned to love and embrace the uniqueness of it. I guess that, for a brief while, I thought that there could really be something special about me: a little, skinny African girl ("skinny" was very early on in my journey, LOL), with nappy, uncontrollable pigtails and a tag that meant I, myself, represented joy. Others were also intrigued by my name. I remember feeling like a movie star when I was in middle school and I was featured in the local newspaper (along with some other classmates) in an article entitled "What's in a Name."

The origin of my name is Nigerian. It derives from the Yoruba tribe and means *love turns to joy*. To say that something "turns to" is symbolic for what happens when one thing is transformed into another. My father was Nigerian but had been in the States to attend school when he met and married my mother. My mother shared with me that in his culture, naming children was done very intentionally. Children were given names that coincided with the family's history, related to their tribal villages, and were based on events that were happening in the lives of the parents at that time. The child's name was often centered around the parents' feelings for each other and the timing of their birth. So when my father abandoned me when I was seven years old and went back to his country, I was confused. His departure planted the first seed of "contradictory love" deep down within my soul. Although I grew to accept the seven-letter word that was slated as my identity, as a child I was unable to reconcile my father's actions with what he had chosen to call me. If their love had turned into joy, why wasn't he happy with me? If he loved me as much as my mom said he did, how could he leave me? If my birth was supposed to bring great pleasure, why did the idea of my existence cause so much pain?

By the time I was twenty years old, the "irreconcilable differences" that had been planted in my childhood had taken root and were starting to grow. I had one kid, my first marriage had fallen apart, and I had begun a relationship with a much older man. This man exposed my life to a different kind of pain. He was unfaithful and mentally and emotionally abusive, and wouldn't hesitate to be physically abusive if I stepped out of what he thought was the line. One night, I was determined to preserve my self-respect by taking a stand. That didn't turn out too well for me, because I ended up slammed into the wall when he picked up my bed and threw it from one side of the room to the other. So as to not rock the abusive boat, I learned to accept that kind of agony as my norm, because it was the exchange for what I thought was love, a love that I so deeply longed for but had never received. He was my cause and cure; the cause of my pain, but the cure to a gaping void. It was a therapeutic yet toxic love. It was a love that left me alone in the abortion clinic twice, and eventually alone through my pregnancy with my second child; after becoming pregnant by him three times, I eventually decided to keep my baby. It was a love that left me center stage in a spotlight that exploited my dysfunction. It finally landed me at a table of people who judged my decisions; their way of holding me accountable was to put me out of the church, the place that I was told would heal me. I will never forget how lost I felt when they sat me down to tell me that my membership was being revoked. They said that it was "obvious that I wasn't going to stop sinning and getting pregnant," so they were no longer accepting me as a part of the congregation. That time in my life dug a deep trench in my soul that shaped how I would see myself for years to come. Not only did I feel rejected by my biological father and by the other men in my life up until that point, being handled that way in the church left me feeling rejected by God. It sent a message to me that my sins were unforgivable, worse than everyone else's, and that I was an embarrassment to those who obviously had no sin and were able to cast the first stone at my life. That I was such an embarrassment that my name, the name that meant "love turns to joy," was not worthy of even existing on the membership roster at the local assembly of believers.

I'm not blaming anyone for my behavior or suggesting that I shouldn't have been held accountable for the consequences of my choices. I'm saying that while my actions appeared to be those of a rebellious "church girl" who was determined to sin against God, underneath was just a little girl who was searching to validate what her father had failed to affirm. I wanted to be loved unconditionally. I needed to be nurtured in grace and healed from the pain that started before I could even make my own choices. I'm saying that being handled according to the "law of religion" broke me into pieces that would take a long time to repair. The way I saw it was that I was being condemned for pursuing something that I deserved. And rather than experience that kind of condemnation again, I deemed myself unworthy of feeling the purity of the deep affection and endearment that most would call love. After that, I spent years struggling in relationships; years of wrestling with my worthiness. I fought to regulate the revolving door of what felt like constant rejection and abandonment. Life felt nothing like my name suggested it would. When I loved, it always turned into pain. My trust turned into constant tears, and my hope for healing became hatred toward those who abused the vulnerability of my desire for true inner peace and supreme satisfaction, of my desire for joy.

Years later, I began to use parts of my story to empower other women to change their perspective on their pain. But even then, it felt like things that were supposed to be good had an adverse effect. One day, while I was riding in the car with my sister, I called the sales manager of the venue that I had rented for my annual empowerment event, as it had dawned on me that I had not heard back from him regarding the return of my rental deposit. He and I had met and completed the walkthrough of the facility after the conference, and he had assured me that I would be receiving my check in the mail, but it still had not arrived. When I reached him on the phone that day, he told me that the "committee" (why does it always have to be blamed on a committee) had met and decided that they were not going to give me my money back.

He claimed that upon further inspection, some crumbs were found on a table. He went on to say that the committee had also found a raffle ticket in the corner on the floor, which to them meant that although we had vacuumed, it was still dirty.

I was infuriated; this made absolutely no sense. A part of me was in disbelief at what was coming out of his mouth. It was definitely a "WTF" (what the freak) moment. My anger superseded the matter at hand. His words agitated everything in me that was mentally exhausted from trying to pursue better. I remember looking at my sister and saying, "Why do I have to fight for everything?" Notice that I used the word *everything* when I was only fighting for one thing. The truth is that I had reached a point where I was just tired of life throwing what felt like unnecessary jabs at me. One of the most dangerous things that you can do is to take what should be an isolated incident and add it to the "pool of pain" that you have been keeping track of and collecting for most of your life. That kind of recordkeeping can cause you to walk away from everything. I was tired of chasing love, tired of seeking happiness, tired of trying to get someone to choose me, tired of not getting what I felt like I deserved, and absolutely sick and tired of people thinking it was okay to mishandle me. That day, it became clear to me how never-ending fatigue, if left unaddressed, can become the reason why even the smallest thing can serve as the proverbial straw that breaks your pain-stricken back.

Now, in case you're wondering what happened to my check, I filed suit and later received what was rightfully mine. But it was never really about the money. This instance became such a relevant part of my story because, as I reflected on how it all unfolded, I heard the words "REMOVE THE FACE" ringing from the unpleasant feeling that I had grown accustomed to feeling in the pit of my stomach. I wanted so badly to launch a "hate campaign" against that man. But the reality is that I had already wasted too many years being angry at people for what they had done to me. Those three words commanded my attention, changed the trajectory of my perspective, and brought about one of the greatest and most important instructions in my life. Regardless of all of my past hurts, ones that went as far back as my childhood, and regardless of who left, who stayed, who inflicted pain, who rejected, who exploited, who laughed, who pointed a finger, who took from me, or who tried to break me, it was imperative that I move on AND forward. Every bit of my journey was designed to teach me something, and now there was a mandate on my life to ignore the faces of those who served as the instructors. I had spent a large portion of my life feeling abandoned by my father and despising anyone who modeled his behavior or whose actions intentionally or unintentionally watered the seed that he had planted in my heart. Now, real growth meant that I needed to extract the lessons and release my anger toward those who were designed to cross my path and teach them. I had to come to terms with the fact that it was never about the people, but always about me being positioned to carry out my true purpose.

Years later, that phrase took on a different meaning; the undertone was much more introspective and the personal challenge became far more intense. It shifted from looking beyond the face of the adversary to removing internal faces that were just as destructive. You see, it's easy for us to pinpoint and recollect what others have done to us, but the game changes substantially when the rulebook requires us to look within. So there I was, front and center with Ifedayo. Reaching the peak of my purpose and continuing to encourage women to pursue theirs would not be possible if I did not submit to the deeper level of mending that needed to take place. I could no longer hide behind the masks of the building blocks that were used to assemble a foundation of painful reference points. "Removing the face" had become a moment of reflection followed by a requirement for transformation. It was about taking off the disguises that were not visible to the naked eye and uncovering that which had been concealed from the inside out. It was about knowing once and for all that the next stop in my change journey would be the place where I would have to acknowledge, but then see past, those formative years of pain. Doing this would connect with the present place in my life where God so desperately wanted to heal me.

My name is "love turns to joy." And I've grown to understand that God's love is capable of bringing me great joy, but in order to truly experience it, I had to be willing to look beyond my pain, search inwardly to see myself differently, and put in the work that was necessary to remove, exchange, and change faces.

If I were asked to offer an ideal manuscript for change, it would be this one with these twelve courageous women, who in the chapters to follow will share their stories and a part of their journeys with you. Each of them will remove the veil of a personal struggle. They will give a voice to the power of change as they share a significant turning point, and they will offer a prescription for pain to those of you who are ready to heal and experience life beyond the hurtful moments that are perhaps keeping you from what's next in your life.

Prescription for the face of pain

My "prescription" for you . . . well, let's just say that it may not be an easy pill to swallow. I encourage you to write down your own story. The first time around, include the names of people who you consider to be the main characters in your narrative of pain. When you are done, rewrite it again. This time, remove the names and replace them with the lessons that each individual taught you. Acknowledge the first story, but then allow the second one to become your new point of reference. This means that your pain has now become your pathway to purpose, and that your adversary will always be a teaching tool and never again a successful opponent. YES! YES! . . . Yes change!

There Is Purpose in the Pit

Shakita Wilson

"Shakita Wilson, you have the right to remain silent. Anything you say or do can and will be held against you in the court of law."

This was the beginning of my "pit" experience. When we hear or even think of the word "pit," there are thoughts of darkness, illness, a rut, no way out, desolation, and every other word that may describe not-so-good feelings. If I was to describe the way I felt during that time, I would say all of the above. Before falling into the pit, I was living a life of what I thought to be the perfect journey to success. I was a single mother and the first in my family to go to college. I was in the process of purchasing my first home and in school finishing up my second degree in criminal justice. I had a great-paying job and had just gotten cleared to work for the secret service—but then, just like that, it was all wiped away within a matter of seconds. On August 1, 2010, I traveled to Atlantic

City, New Jersey, to celebrate my daughter's twelfth birthday, and before I knew it, I was getting my Miranda Rights read to me and was thrown into a jail cell.

The day started out so beautiful. We went to Sunday worship, then hurried home to get our bags so we could hit the highway. It was a warm, sunny afternoon full of laughter and plans for sightseeing during our stay. As we arrived at the hotel, it began to get dark outside. My daughter was so excited because of the bright lights; I couldn't tell which was shining the brightest, the lights or her big, beautiful smile. As we hurried to get checked in to begin the festivities, I allowed the valet attendant to park my car. After check-in we took our bags to the room, then decided to take a stroll on the boardwalk. As we began to head out of the huge glass sliding doors of the hotel, I saw my car with all of the doors opened, along with the trunk, and, to top it off, surrounded by police officers.

I approached one of the officers to see if everything was okay, and he asked me, "Is this your vehicle?"

I said yes and the officer asked me if I was aware I had a firearm in my vehicle. I answered, "Oh, yes, that's mine, I have a license for it." He gave me a very harsh look and told me he needed me to come with him to the police station for questioning.

As a person who worked really closely with law enforcement, I knew that going to the police station meant hours of questioning and possibly having to stay for a while. As I sat in the back of the smelly police car, un-handcuffed, I still had my cellphone, so I called my daughter to let her know everything was going to be okay, and to tell her how much I loved her and that I would see her soon. I thanked God there was another adult and child with my daughter to keep her occupied in my absence.

Eventually I arrived at the station and was placed in a small room for over two hours of being questioned about the firearm in my vehicle. I explained that it was a honest mistake, and that the intent was never to bring the firearm with me on vacation, that I had been in a rush to start the celebration of my daughter's birthday. There were two cops; I thought of them as the bad cop, who yelled and screamed when he talked, and then the good cop, who spoke with a mellow tone. After hours of questioning I was charged and placed under arrest for the possession of an unregistered firearm in the state of New Jersey.

Never in a million years would I have ever imagined being on the other side of the justice system. I called my daughter to let her know that I loved her and I would see her in a few hours. I then contacted my parents to let them know what all had happened and that I would be in contact with them as soon as I was released. The officer escorted me to this tiny jail cell and had me remove my belt, jewelry, and shoelaces to assure I would not attempt to commit suicide. As I walked into that tiny space, a room that had a steel bunkbed with the toilet and water fountain connected, the door buzzed and slammed behind me, and as the officer proceeded to walk off, he said that as long as my background came back clean, I would be released. As I sat at the edge of the bed waiting to be released, all I could think about was my baby girl.

After being booked and fingerprinted, my mugshot taken and my background checked and cleared, I was finally released after almost twelve hours. The officer came and unlocked the door, gave me a brown paper bag with my belongings, and literally opened the back door to the jail to let me out, then shut it after me. There I was, with no sense of direction of where to go, and my cellphone was dead. As I started walking, I heard a little voice say "Mommy!" and all I could do was cry; my daughter and everyone had stayed in the car in the parking lot at the jail until I was released.

I couldn't leave the state of New Jersey until I went before the judge. Let's just say that that was truly "the vacation from hell." As the vacation went on, I had to mask my feelings of fear of the unknown in front of my daughter because I had to keep on smiling and giving her the reassurance that everything was going to be okay. I found myself going into the bathroom every chance I got to cry, and I kept my sunshades on to hide my puffy eyes.

The court date finally arrived, and I had no idea what to expect as the judge began to read my charge before the court. It was the recommendation of the prosecutor that I remain in custody in New Jersey until my court date, since I was not a resident and was thus a potential flight risk. My entire heart fell into my stomach. Fortunately, the judge denied the recommendation of the prosecutor. After I was given my court date, I walked out of that courtroom, jumped in the car, and got on the highway back to Richmond so fast that I'm sure I drove well above the speed limit trying to get as far away from Jersey as possible.

During that time, the position I held at a financial institution required random background checks, and because I'm an upfront, honest person, I let my employer know about the charge. Their response was to keep them posted on the outcome. I was thinking that at least my employer would be understanding, and that everything was going to be okay.

After months and months of anticipation, the sentencing date arrived. I was charged with a felony and sentenced to serve one year probation in Richmond, Virginia, with a one hundred thirty five dollar court cost fee. There I was, a convicted felon at the age of thirty-one, having never once been caught up in the justice system before, in trouble. I would be remiss if I said I wasn't angry. I didn't get any fines for the unregistered firearm, but I received a felony charge with court costs. I'm sure it could've been much worse, but to me the punishment just didn't fit the crime.

I followed up with my employer to let them know the outcome—and, needless to say, for the first time ever in life I was let go from a job. I just couldn't believe what I was hearing. I asked the manager to repeat what he said. My direct manager, who was also in the room, couldn't hold back the tears. I was in disbelief, feeling numb; I just set my badge on the table and walked out of the room.

My daughter and I were already staying with my parents because I had just relocated from North Carolina; it looked like we would be staying with them a bit longer than planned. I began applying for jobs and received rapid responses back for interviews, but once the potential employers learned about the felony conviction I was no longer up for consideration. After being told no over and over again, I knew I had to do something different. I decided to go to hair school; since hair had always been a hobby of mine, why not make it a career?

I started hair school with twenty-two people in my class and ended with seven. I was the first to graduate amongst my peers. I took the state board test, both written and practical, and received passing scores—only to later receive a letter saying, "At this time we are not able to issue you a cosmetology license in the state of Virginia due to a felony conviction on your record." In order to be considered, I had to go to a panel hearing. There I was again, back at square one, dumped into a dark hole with my hands tied together and thrown against the wall. Nine months and two panel hearings later, I was granted my cosmetology license. By that time I was two and a half years into experiencing unemployment and living on government assistance, receiving food stamps.

After receiving my cosmetology license, I started working as a hairstylist at a local chain salon. Mind you, the hustle didn't match the dollar because of the commission-based salary. This barely placed a dollar in my pocket and food on the table, and the food stamps had been shut off. But finally I had some good fortune: I applied for a job at a high-end insurance company that overlooked the felony conviction and gave me a chance. Looka hea, I was one happy sistah! I felt as if there was still hope and I could begin to breathe again.

Now that you've had an opportunity to journey through my experience in the pit, I want you to journey with me through my purpose. As I look back over what I call the seven year "pit," I can humbly say that it was worth it and that I'm most grateful. How so? It's because, in going into that deep, dark, scary place of my life, I was able to discover my strength. This experience allowed me to discover my purpose, and at the end of the day it was necessary. Through it all I never gave up and I kept fighting. Because of the fight, I was able to get a pardon from the governor of New Jersey after seven long years, with all of my rights restored. I currently have a hair salon named Glam Boxx by KiWi, LLC, home of "Healthy Head Turning Looks." I currently hold public office as a notary for the Commonwealth of Virginia. I'm a contracted notary signing agent accredited with the National Notary Association. I've also taken my experience and used it to birth The RUTH Foundation (Redeemed Under The Holy Spirit), a pre-entry/post-entry nonprofit organization geared toward individuals who have encountered the criminal justice system and who are seeking another chance. It also allows me to volunteer weekly at the local jails, where I mentor and encourage women serving their prison sentences. I NEVER in a million years would've or could've imagined accepting the call as a minister of the gospel of Jesus Christ without this necessary experience.

So, my sister or brother, when you are faced with life's challenges, I want you to get all of the emotions out, whether it be through crying, screaming, kicking, or venting, and then take a deep breath. Some experiences will be more traumatic than others, and we must pause and remind ourselves that such experiences are necessary.

Prescription for the pain of the pit

When the pain is so heavy you can no longer bear it alone, you must:

1. Connect with a strong support system, positive influences who will encourage you and pull you out of the pit. I thank God for my support system, who were my family and true friends. Take note that I said "true" friends, because some will fall away, but the loyal ones will stick around.

2. Choose a positive word and recite it to yourself daily, as often as possible throughout the day. My word is HOPE, which simply means a feeling of expectation and desire for a certain thing to happen.

3. When some days are tougher than others, shift your focus onto something positive. For me, I thought about how my daughter's face would light up when she's eating ice cream with sprinkles.

4. Start journaling your thoughts of what life will be like once you're out of the dark place.

These are a few pain prescriptions to reference when you're having a bad day or just feel like throwing in the towel. I pray that this has encouraged you and has given you hope and the will to fight to continue the journey into your purpose. My hope is that at least one pain prescription will be able to help you, and that you will be able to add your own to the list to encourage others that may be going through, or who may even have already gone through, similar situations. I pray my journey has inspired and encouraged you to fight and push yourself out of the pit into your purpose. Remember, you are never alone, especially with the right support team and the courage to move forward. God bless you and the amazing journey ahead.

A Look Through the Looking Glass

Kiara Washington

The only thing I know is that I know nothing at all. With all that I thought that I knew, I have come to realize that nothing is for certain, and that if I rely on my expectations of others I will lose every time.

Fear has crept into the makings of this process. Fear has whispered in my ear and has shown me that it is present with me. Nonetheless, whether fear has decided to show its ugly head or not, I have still decided to proceed forth with this mandate that has been placed upon my life.

Where do I start? The only place I know where to start is from the beginning.

I was born and raised humbly in the county of Henrico, a small county outside of Richmond, Virginia. In the winter of 1990, my twin brother Keith and I made our entrance into this world. We were not our parents' first sets of pride and joy. Before our debut, our older siblings Kevin and Christina were already in existence.

Better believe that with three other siblings there was never one dull moment, especially for my mother. My mother raised us with structure and discipline. Things had to be done a certain way, by a certain time, and with a certain attitude. This is something I am sure she was taught by her mother, my grandmother Geraldine Johnson, affectionately known as "Gama."

Now, my grandmother Ms. Geraldine Johnson was not someone to take lightly. She raised three children on her own: my mother, my aunt Vicki, and my uncle William. There was no assistance from my grandfather, according to my grandmother. To be perfectly honest, I do not even know my grandfather's name. Talk about the "missing pieces" to the family tree.

No matter, and no criticism handed out to anyone for the loss of information. As a true optimist, I've come to find it more beneficial for me to find the positive that exists in every situation. I do, however, believe that if I would have had the opportunity to meet my grandfather, my perspective on men in general would have been different.

In the twenty-nine years I have been alive, I've come to learn that when we are granted the opportunity to create certain relationships, whether those be the relationships with our fathers, mothers, grandmothers, or grandfathers, we develop insight on what those relationships should look like. However, when we have not been afforded that luxury, there is no guiding light for us to follow.

Here is the good news: we are in control of our own lives. We have the ability to reshape and recreate our lives at any given time. I already know what your next question is: Well, Kiara, how *do* I reshape or recreate my life, especially when it seems the one I have been given isn't currently going too well?

Well, allow me to give you a quick, transparent look through my personal life. It's a life that at one time or another was so upside down and so confused, I was not sure if I was coming or going. I was a gifted soul with no true guidance or mentoring. I was so lost, with no real idea of how lost I truly was.

As I mentioned previously, I am one of four children. My mother, like so many other mothers in this world, raised her children without a consistent father figure to guide them. I could bore you with all of the stories and details about how my father was absent and was "too busy running the streets," but I will not do that. Instead, I'll explain to you how his absence helped me find my purpose.

Did you know that pain can help create purpose? I was not aware of this as a young child; neither was I aware of this as a teenager. I just knew that it hurt to be a statistic. My mother did the best she knew how to do with four children; however, we could see and feel as children that she was completely overwhelmed by life. We watched her struggle time and time again to provide for us growing up. We grew up in the church, so we became quite accustomed to the traditional black church "love offerings" on Sundays. Even though I had clothes on my back and there was always food on the table (which I was grateful for), I could not help but feel depressed by this cycle of never having enough. I wondered, for long periods of my life, where was this feeling coming from?

I looked at the previous generation before my mother and saw the detrimental cycle. It all then began to make sense. My mother had subconsciously seen this behavior modeled before her as a child. Her mother, my grandmother, was a hard-working woman who had also taken care of three children by herself.

So then I began to ask myself, why does it seem that the women I have been raised by have chosen partners who have chosen not to stick around? Partners who have chosen not to take care of their responsibilities? Partners who have pretended for years on end that they did not help create life in this world?

I had no answers for these questions as a young child or teenager, but as I have become older I have figured out the answers. Remember how earlier in this chapter I mentioned the importance of key relationships growing up? A prime example is that a household that contains both mother and father will give the children that they are raising the example of how to be loved by each parent, as well as the basic structures of how to be a parent. When both roles of mother and father are present in a child's life, it can make all the difference in the world.

The woman who raised me had her mother, but did not have her father. The woman who raised my mother did not have her mother, nor did she have her father; instead, my grandmother was raised by her grandparents. These two generations did not experience direct love and care from the beings who were supposed to be the two essential people in their lives.

Imagine trying to teach something you're not quite familiar with yourself. Imagine the challenges that you may face. Can you already see the mistakes that you may make, trying to show someone something you have little to no experience in yourself? My guess is that you would struggle at it miserably. You may also add things that are incorrect or take away parts that may be needed.

The fact that my grandmother, mother, and I shared the same experience of not having our fathers present in our lives speaks volumes. It means that the three of us have missed out on vital information while growing up, which also means we have had to fill in the missing pieces along the way. This, in my experience, has been a recipe for disaster. We all needed more help.

I used to cry for my father late in the night. As a child, teenager, and young adult, I was involved in many activities that I wished he could have witnessed and been a part of. I always wanted him to know how naturally talented and gifted I was. His absence created a major disconnect with the male species in my life. I had no idea as to how the minds of men worked. I struggled with knowing and understanding my full worth, and because of this I endured major heartbreaks in my youth.

The day that turned my life around was December 11, 2017. After that day my life was never the same. On that day, after a battle with cancer, my beautiful mother transitioned into her new life in heaven. As relieved as I was to not see her suffering in pain anymore, my heart and soul still felt as though they were torn apart. I felt like most folks do when they lose somebody they love dearly: I wished I had more time. I realized that for the first time in my life I was without both of my parents. The guidance that I was once used to receiving from my mother was no longer present in my life. I felt completely and utterly alone. Through this sadness and grief, I was compelled to change my life. I was not sure of how to begin this change, but I was willing to figure it out!

Here is how I know for certain my mother's death changed me: not only could I see it, but everyone else around me could see the change as well. Her abrupt transition ignited a fire within me. I managed to see that throughout her life, she was a gifted and sometimes misunderstood soul. However, after her death I began to see her power. I also began to see that everything that she so deeply desired had been lying in plain sight. She just had not stepped up and seized it.

I also began to look within my own self. I began to search my mind, heart, and soul for my life's purpose. Her death created such an impact in my life. After her death, I decided to begin sharing that impact with others around me in hopes that my words and experiences would help them rise up and out. I stopped running away from my pain and began to run toward it.

I could have decided to waste time feeling sorry for myself. I could have decided to cave in and chosen to not deal with the hurt and pain. I could have decided to totally give up. After all, I did feel alone. I had people around me, but no parents. No guiding light. My father, who is still living, has consistently chosen to not participate in my life. At almost thirty years old I have still found myself wondering why he has chosen to not be a part of my life. But I have also realized that I will never know the real answer. Moreover, it is my job as a consciously aware woman to affirm myself every single day, regardless of if I was or was not afforded this luxury from both of my parents as a young child. What I could not afford to do anymore was sulk and assign blame. This storm in my life, I have come to realize, was just a part of the process.

In fighting through the pain of loss and abandonment, I became more determined than ever! I began listening to other great entrepreneurs, speakers, and mentors. I launched two businesses in less than a year, and paid off all of my credit card debt! I had goals and I was on a roll!

Suddenly, however, in April of 2019, I discovered that I too had a large tumor that had developed on my left kidney. After all the self-work and self-healing I had done, I now had to deal with cancer at twenty-nine years old?! Now that was a hard pill to swallow, especially since the day before I was diagnosed I was totally "fine," or at least felt fine. After being admitted to the hospital, and while the doctors were figuring out what should be done (do we leave the kidney or do we take it?), all I could think about was my mother. I thought about how she battled cancer twice in her lifetime. I also began to think about my grandmother, and how she battled cancer as well. I then began to look at myself and realized something so plain and simple: It is a MUST that I take better care myself. How ironic is it that I had just lost my mom to cancer not even two years prior to fighting the same battle myself?

It was a glimpse through the looking glass. I, for the first time, saw myself standing in the exact same place my mother had been standing in. And in the midst of the storm, I felt such a sense of peace, one that I am not sure I could even explain. It is true that the Creator will give us peace in the midst of the storm. As I have grown and matured throughout my lifetime, I have come to find out that all of the things that look as though they were sent to hurt me were, in hindsight, only sent to build me up and strengthen me for my destiny. Therefore, for everything that seemed to rise up against me, it was all working for my good. Throughout this battle God had already assured me of my future healing.

You know, in the beginning of 2019 I had a serious conversation with God. I said something to the effect of this: "God, I am tired of playing small. I desire the life that you have for me. I choose to become intentional about my life. I know that I may have been born into poverty and neglected at a young age by my father, and I have made multiple mistakes, but I know that I am still worthy of purpose."

When I tell you the universe heard me loud and clear, I mean that it heard me loud and clear! This is the thing: when we speak out into the universe, it is already done. So we must act and believe as if it is already done. This is the power of manifesting the life that we say we want and so badly desire.

There is power in the words that we say. Throughout my brief battle with cancer I learned yet another valuable lesson, that no matter our age, none of us are invincible. Life can and will happen to us all, and sometimes without signs or warning.

Here and now I stand before you, cancer-free, more loving, more dedicated, and far more intentional about my life! I may have lost my mother, the most important person in the world to me, but I am still here. My father may not ever become a part of my life, but that's all right. I may only have one kidney, but I am alive. Since I am still alive and breathing, my life still has purpose, and it is up to me to fulfill it. Before deciding to write this chapter, I remember feeling myself stepping into something new. It was frightening, but exhilarating at the same time. In hindsight, my upbringing has given me perspective. My father's absence has made me stronger. My mother's death has made me intentional. Lastly, growing up in poverty has made me aware and determined to never repeat the cycle again.

Prescription for breaking the cycle of generational curses

1. Start with yourself. There is nothing going on out in the world that we can help fix or repair unless we decide to do the internal work within ourselves first.

2. Stop blaming others for your current state. No matter who has walked away, you still have a purpose to fulfill.

3. Be aware of your energy and surroundings. We become most like the things and people we spend our time with.

Use these three steps daily and you will activate the new you that the world has been waiting for. Go out and create your best life!

This Is Not Your Assignment

Lynnetta M. Seabury

Hello . . . My name is Lynnetta . . . and I AM NO LONGER A FEAR ADDICT.

My addiction to fear started in my mid-twenties. I am a pastor's daughter who grew up in a sheltered environment believing in and loving God with my whole heart. Even though church folk tend to have certain expectations of how a pastor's child should act—that they must love everybody, attend church daily, and sing "Kumbaya my Lord" instead of "I want to sex you up"—the sheltered life that I was living became an issue, and I wanted to escape to the forbidden world. I was ready to live and to taste the banned fruit that seemed to me to be delicious. I ended up becoming a wife, and once I left my parents' home, I began to realize I was able to do ANYTHING, and I was ready. During the early stages of my marriage, I started acting in live stage productions, and I met an older man that swept me off my unstable feet. Since

I was a new resident in this world of freedom, the scent I left in the air was just like a wounded sea creature that was left for a shark to devour. Before I knew it, I was having an affair.

I began to pull away from my family, my old friends, and, most importantly, God. No one could convince me that I was wrong, because I was in love, or should I say in lust. I ended up living with the ill-gotten gains of the world and my life began to change. One Sunday, I decided to visit my parents at church, and my mom wanted to converse with me alone. As she was talking, she began to cry and explained that God had woken her up out of a sound sleep, and she needed to tell me what God had told her. I listened for the inflections in her voice, which gave me the cue to say, "yes, ma'am." As my mom transferred her heart to me, she said this phrase: "you will die if you don't leave him alone." The word *die* flooded my mind so heavily that I began to feel drops of tears collecting on my cheeks. I remember looking up and saying I *don't* want to die. At that very second, the possibility of dying became so real. I immediately ended the affair with the "lust" of my life and moved forward. I knew then that this new-found fear wasn't supposed to be a part of my journey, so I placed the fear deep in the crevices of my mind and tried to forget it.

When I finally made it to the great forties, fear began to creep back into my life. My family and I relocated to a new state, and I began desperately searching for friendship, a sisterhood. After we joined a local church, I met a group of women that I knew would be my East Coast Sisters, and we started a business together. Months later, though, the business and the friendships disintegrated. I was devastated, and began to feel fear slowly creeping behind me as if to overtake my mind, body, and soul. I began to feel a deep sense of loss, grief, as if each of them had died. I openly mourned and found it difficult to get past the hurt and the pain. I thought I had packed away those feelings, but it seemed as if I had slowly begun to reopen the luggage that was neatly packed away into the crevices of my mind. No matter how I tried to avoid this fear, it continued to make appointments with me daily that I couldn't break.

Let me clarify this fear to you, my friends. My fear is not people, animals, or leaving the house; my fear is dying. Believe it not, a significant loss for me triggers the fear of dying, even when that loss has nothing to do with death. I grieve the loss, and then a realization (which is not a true reality) causes me to embrace the thoughts of dying. There are days that this enslavement is so strong that it causes physical pain. I *form* the symptoms, I *feel* the symptoms, and I *fear* the symptoms.

In the year 2015, the form of the symptoms became so prevalent in my life that thoughts of death began to flood my mind daily. My grandmother, whom I loved so dearly, had transitioned from earth to heaven. My grandmother was a woman of peace but would put you in your place if needed. I remember once attending a wedding with my granny, and all we could do was look at each other and smile; the smile for me was a smile of pain, but her smile was a reminder that everything was okay. The wedding we were attending was officiated by my father and coordinated by my mom, and my siblings were participants in the wedding. You see, the bride was my so-called "best friend" and the groom was my ex-boyfriend. Technically, I should have not attended this day of "bliss," but my grandmother said she would be my plus one and that all would be fine. We attended the wedding, and no, I didn't attend the reception. After we left the wedding, Granny allowed me to fall and cry in her arms as I grieved the loss of those who I once loved with all my heart.

As time went by, my grandmother was diagnosed with Parkinson's Disease. An individual who has this disease can experience tremors, problems swallowing, and constant pain. I got the opportunity to see my grandmother in that state, and after our visit I began to feel as if I was experiencing the same symptoms. If I saw the slightest tremor, I automatically diagnosed myself with Parkinson's. Even though my grandmother was constantly saying she was doing fine, I took on the pain that I knew she was feeling. I would research each sign and would pride myself in my self-diagnosing skills. It didn't matter where the pain would arise, I immediately interpreted the pain as the crippling disorder which would lead to death. In my mind, the symptoms were very real and the terror I was feeling left me helpless and hopeless.

The mere thought of losing my grandmother became so real to me that the grieving started before she died. I knew I was about to lose the lady who convinced me to not get a perm anymore. The lady who made the best gumbo on this side of heaven. The lady who would sing happy birthday to me every birthday. I was on the verge of NEVER seeing her again; once more, I unpacked fear.

My family and I had always dreamed of owning our own home, and around that time we finally had the opportunity to do so. When that moment finally arrived, the entire household was excited. You could feel the excitement pouring out of the door every time the doorbell would ring. Friends and family were visiting us and saying how happy they were for us—but on the inside, I was afraid of becoming a homeowner and what it would entail. I began to feel fear and would experience panic attacks daily. There were numerous times that the paramedics were called, only for the feeling of dying to subside as soon as they would enter the door. I would wake up from a dead sleep and would tell my husband that I needed to go to the hospital NOW! Even though I knew that the trip to the emergency room would disturb my entire household, I didn't care. I needed to get there so I could make sure I was healthy and not dying. I would spend many hours in my own head, counseling myself as if I were a professional counselor. I just couldn't wrap my head around why this was happening and why I was continuing to feel the fear of death. I had spoken words of encouragement to others and it worked for them. It's ironic that I could converse with others and advise them, but was unable to speak into my own life; I did not believe anything I had to say for myself!

It was obvious that family and friends could see my pain and tried to help, but I was reluctant to receive their comfort. The fear was mine, and I needed to nurture it, and nothing anyone would say could make a difference. I feared dying so much that I would sleep sitting straight up. During this time, I dreamed one night that I was in a bedroom talking to my sister. The scene changed to me seeing and feeling that I was dying. I called out to my sister and she never responded. My breath became shallow and I watched myself take my last breath. This dream terrorized me so much that I couldn't lay flat in bed. If I did sleep in the bed, my position was upright and upright only. In the morning, though, I would wake up and find myself laying down, as if God had taken His hands and laid me down gently. My dreams were controlling my life, and I would allow my nightmares to send me into a mental place where I would attempt to do everything possible to live. My feelings were real, and I was fighting for my life. As months passed, I would wake in anticipation that the day was going to be great, but then night would appear and the darkness of the night would cause the terror of death to overtake my mind, body, and soul; I did not want to lay down.

I began to read the Scriptures and pray diligently because my life depended on each minute and second of my time with God. I placed a note in my bathroom that stated: "I am less, God is more." The more I would pray and seek God, the more the dark places began to be filled with light. I physically started seeing changes in my daily living. I once again neatly packed away my fear of death and began to breathe and live each day with hope.

But then the cycle began once again (I know . . . *again*), and this time I needed everyone to fear the symptoms with me. I would call my sisters and explain to them what I was experiencing at that moment. If they couldn't talk right away and needed to call me back, I would hold the phone in my hands and wait for their call. I would send pictures of the current issue and would blow the image up so they could see the area of concern. I even called my mom, who happens to be a nurse, and would seek medical attention and advice from her. It got to the point that she said, "Do not call me anymore with your so-called health problems; call your doctor." The sternness in her voice resonated so deeply in my mind that I had to take a step back and realize that I had fully unpacked the fear and the multiple thoughts of dying once more.

One day after that call, my sons and I were on our way home from school, and we were discussing what we were going to eat for dinner. Every day I would take this route home from the school, and to us it was a normal day. I could hear my sons laughing at each other's choices, and I would often glance at them in the rearview mirror just to make eye contact with them. As I came to an intersection and a stoplight, the sunlight suddenly appeared strongly from behind the trees. All I heard from the backseat was, "Mom, we are going to hit that truck!" Many thoughts began to flood my mind: I can't be dying, the boys are in the car. They are too young to die; I am too young to die. Oh God, death was finally looking me straight in the face and there was nothing I could do! I couldn't stop the car from hitting the truck. I couldn't get the boys or myself out of the car quick enough to avoid impact. I grabbed the steering wheel and instead embraced the impact. The airbag immediately deployed and the car was filled with smoke. I quickly turned around to make sure that the boys were okay, and they began to scream and cry. My oldest screamed out, "Mom, you are bleeding!" At that very moment, that very second, I realized that I had to leave my fear of dying at that place. God showed me that I would never be able to stop death; when it's my time, it'll be my time. I must truly believe that He is in control. I didn't lose my life, I didn't lose my children; we are alive, and not only alive, but alive and well.

There are days that I still have a faceoff with fear, but I know that God has not given me the spirit of fear, but of love, power, and a sound mind. Since God has not given me the spirit of fear, it is evident that fear is not my assignment. I am convinced that I must rely on the love of God, the love of my family and friends, and the love I have for myself. Since God has given me power, I have the power to overcome the feelings of fear. The power that God has instilled in me is a daily reminder that I can do all things through Christ who strengthens me. Therefore, I have power over my thoughts and insecurities that arise daily. Finally, with a sound mind, I can address the fears that try to overtake my life.

I want to encourage you, my friend, that whatever has consumed your life and caused you to fear, you don't have to feed that fear anymore. If you need to post notes of affirmation in and around your home, office, or car to make it through the day, it's okay. We are all trying to manage this life with the tools we have inside of us and the tools that have been placed at our disposal. We are coping, we are surviving, we are leaning on the power of Christ and on each other for strength. Just as the words of life and hope were spoken into my being, I declare to you, my friend: "Fear is not your assignment."

Prescription for the foul smell of fear

To overcome fear, LIVE! Learn to live and realize that you are not alone; others are experiencing the same thing, so don't be afraid to talk about it. Connect yourself with people who will refuse to let you or your dream die. Isolation is the tool that fear uses to keep you unpacking the things that keep you bound. Stop unpacking, because fear is not your assignment.

Live, my friend, live well!

I Didn't Know
My Own Strength

Sandra L. Parker

I didn't know my own strength. As I look back over my life, I didn't know how strong I was. I didn't fully understand at the time that many of the challenges I endured would be necessary in order for me to find my strength and propel me into my purpose. I didn't feel strong, and the more I endured life's challenges, the more I felt anything but strong. It's hard to be strong when life throws one curveball after another. It's a difficult thing to be strong when your hopes and dreams never come to fruition. And how do you muster up enough strength to keep fighting when your life resembles failure no matter how you look at it? Oftentimes, family and friends would tell me how much they admired my strength. But I was tired, and for the life of me I couldn't see the strength that was inside of me. While those around me found it easy to place the "strong woman" label on me, I couldn't embrace it. For me, I was simply living day to day, existing in what I describe as survival mode.

I didn't know my own strength. These words are the title to a song that my favorite artist, Whitney Houston, recorded in 2009. I recently listened to these words again and they resonated with me so deeply:

- Survived my darkest hour
- My faith kept me alive
- I picked myself back up
- Hold my head up high
- I was not built to break
- I didn't know my own strength.

Much like Ms. Houston, I lived much of my life without realizing my strength. There were many challenges that I never saw coming, but I managed to survive. My first marriage ended in divorce and forced me into single motherhood. Being a single mother, having to decide whether to eat or keep the lights on, hardly sounded strong to me. Living with a space heater in one room because there wasn't enough money to heat the entire house didn't sound like a person with strength. To me it had everything to do with survival.

I lost my mother to a heart attack when I was only seven years old. Seven years later, my father succumbed to cirrhosis of the liver. I survived the lack of nurturing that I saw most of my friends receiving, and I survived the fact that I would never fully be the daddy's girl that I always dreamt I would be. Up until that time, no one had ever taught me how to be strong, so the easiest thing for me was to keep surviving. Even at the age of twenty-six, as I made funeral arrangements for my grandparents, who had died twenty-eight days apart, I kept telling myself that if I could survive this, I would be fine.

Survival was normal for me. After all, how could I break down and die when the life of my beautiful daughter was in my hands? So, through every heartbreak, disappointment, failure, and pain, I survived because I didn't give up.

I had not healed. I was holding on to unresolved pain and I didn't know how to ask for what I needed. Asking for help was out of the question, because those that I believed were supposed to help me had either died, abandoned me, or betrayed me. I knew about prayer, but it never seemed to work. But then, one day, it hit me to pray a more specific prayer. I prayed for strength. I had no idea that what was about to happen in my life would require strength I didn't know I possessed. It would require strength to live when I didn't want to.

Imagine hearing the words "you are unattractive" from the man that had been your husband for five years. After being confronted about his recent infidelity, he chose those words to answer the question, "Why did you cheat?" While that was about thirteen years ago now, I will never forget hearing those words that cut me so deeply. Words that forced me to second-guess the person I thought I was. Words that became the root of the self-hatred I suffered for years.

I was a thirty-eight-year-old wife of a dark, not-so-tall, handsome man that I considered to be my soul mate. After meeting through a mutual friend, we both felt a connection and fell deeply in love. It didn't take long to know that we were meant for each other, and in less than a year I found myself walking down the aisle to be the wife that I had pictured as a little girl.

As I walked down the aisle on March 31, 2001, streams of tears rolled down my face. Family and friends stood with smiling faces as I strolled closer to the man that would soon become my husband. What they didn't know, however, is that he wasn't my soul mate, and the tears that I couldn't keep from falling were because I KNEW I was making a big mistake. I loved him, but deep down I knew he was not the man for me.

It was too late to call off the wedding. Too much had been invested in that day. With handsome groomsmen and beautiful bridesmaids all assembled, I couldn't find the strength to stop what I knew was a huge mistake. Instead, I kept my arm tightly linked with my brother's as he continued to walk me closer to the man who would hurt me, but who also would unknowingly help me discover the strength that had been deeply hidden for years.

Following the wedding and honeymoon, my fears were lessened, as being married didn't seem so bad. We worked diligently to coordinate our schedules as we learned to find ways to live as husband and wife. For the most part he was a good husband, and I thought I was doing a good job at being a good wife. Could it have been nerves that had caused my dread? Maybe it was just all of the planning and preparation in making sure things were perfect. Aside from the normal couple spats, things were working out and we both were loving the married life.

We celebrated a couple of wonderful anniversaries—but the third year proved to be different. Slowly, the loving husband that I had grown accustomed to became a distant, angry man. Though I made several attempts to get answers, he would never give me any. I even thought of ways to blame myself and beg for his forgiveness, promising to be a better wife. But he made it clear that he wanted a divorce.

Divorce number two was inevitable. I was embarrassed and felt like a failure. I found myself alone (again) with no real explanation as to why. I cringed at the questions I knew would follow, but not having the answers made matters even worse.

Those three words, "you are unattractive," haunted me for years. After all that time healing from one failed marriage, I felt my heart was being crushed all over again, and I couldn't imagine how I could recover. The man that had vowed to love me forever, no matter what, had spewed out hateful words that ripped my heart and spirit to pieces. I internalized those words over and over again.

In the midst of my divorce, I felt the urge to make a change. I didn't have all the details and I couldn't fully verbalize what I was feeling, but I knew it would require something major. It wasn't long before I discovered that that major thing would be me moving three thousand miles away to the state of California.

I didn't move right away, but I couldn't ignore what I knew had to be done. After sharing my thoughts and feelings with my brother and a friend, I made the necessary arrangements to leave my home; my daughter and I packed our clothes and boarded a plane to what would be our new home for the next sixteen months. With no job and very little money, I had no idea what to expect. I prayed that we would be okay, and deep down inside I felt that we would be. I didn't have to worry about housing because my brother had opened his home to us and made sure we didn't need a thing. I was also grateful that my daughter seemed to be adjusting to all of the sudden changes.

I still had more questions than answers. What about a car? How long would it take to find employment? How would the bills get paid? What I knew for sure was that the money I had wouldn't last very long. I continued to pray, and deep down, I believed that God was going to take care of us.

I stayed close to God and prayed daily. I journaled daily as well—but one morning in particular was different. As I began to write about my insecurities, my anger about the divorce, my fears, and even my self-hatred, I felt an overwhelming sense of peace. There were no feelings of guilt, but rather an inner peace that reassured me that I was going to be okay. On that particular morning, I felt God's presence in a way I'd never felt before.

As I basked in His presence, God whispered softly, "You are the apple of my eye." Those words altered my life, and suddenly things began to shift. I started thinking differently. My writing changed. As I journaled, I looked for ways to encourage myself. The more I wrote, the more it became apparent that my words could no longer be confined to the pages of the journal. There was a story to be told. In my spirit, I kept hearing that it was a story of strength. But how could I write about strength when I didn't feel strong? But I continued to write, and in 2006, I shared my story of strength as I published "A New Vue," a newsletter written to encourage, motivate, and inspire women.

That name, "A New Vue," was chosen to help me see differently. For years I convinced myself that I was living in survival mode, but the truth was that I was strong. I just didn't know my own strength. So, "A New Vue" was the manifestation of God showing me just how strong I was. Doors began to open, and I was asked to place my newsletters in a local barbershop. I also mailed them to my family and friends back in Virginia. After receiving a copy of the newsletters, one friend wrote, "I loved to read them. Please do not ever stop empowering women like me, I appreciate you."

The culmination of everything that has happened in my story has revealed to me just how strong I am. I lost so much, yet I gained so much more. I lost husbands, family, and friends along the way, and I endured many painful situations, but I learned how to give myself grace to move past my pain.

There was purpose in my pain. I believe that I survived my pain because there was more to my life than I ever imagined. God knew this day would come. He knew that the dark moments, the valley experiences, the pain and disappointments would be the conduit to propel me into something greater. "I didn't know my own strength" aren't just words to a song, they're a story of how survival manifests into a story of strength.

I believe that my strength came to full fruition when Speak Life on Purpose, LLC, a women's empowerment movement, was born. It is a movement that provides the opportunity for me to encourage others on a daily basis. My desire to live and encourage others wasn't easy, but it was a part of the process of becoming who I am today.

Life will always throw curveballs. Sooner or later, we will all endure a blow that seems to take the life out of us. But you don't have to let your situation or the place you find yourself in get the best of you. There is a reason that I didn't break—even though I felt like it. I may have crashed down and tumbled, but I didn't crumble. Just as I survived my darkest hours, you will too.

Finding my strength came at a cost. I lost my joy and peace. My identity was stolen. I didn't recognize the person I saw in the mirror day after day. My sense of worth and my self-love were stripped without my permission, and I didn't know how to fight back and reclaim those things that were lost and stolen from me. Until . . .

Until . . . I reconciled the fact that the process of finding my strength would include going back and reclaiming everything that was taken from me. But how do you reclaim joy, peace, and self-love? How do reclaim your strength from the pain that made you weak? How do you forgive yourself and move forward?

Prescription for the welts of weakness

There are so many ways to reclaim things that you lost in the midst of trying to survive. I survived, and I want you to survive as well. I'd like to leave you with a few prescriptions that I believe will be helpful in your quest to heal the pain points that you may be enduring now or in the future:

1. **Learn to love yourself (again).** Self-love is all about recognizing and affirming who you are. Loving yourself helps you take better care of yourself. When you learn to love yourself, you won't have time to compare yourself to others; instead, you'll learn to embrace everything about you. Practice repeating daily affirmations on self-love. Affirmations are a good way to liberate yourself while eliminating negative self-talk.

2. **Find your tribe.** Surround yourself with people who love and support you. Your tribe will lift you up and encourage you to see the beautiful person that you are. Your tribe will challenge you, but also inspire you. Your tribe won't allow you to play small; they will push you to be the best you that you can be.

3. **Give yourself grace.** Don't be so hard on yourself. Make a conscious effort every single day to forgive yourself. Give yourself the grace and time you need to move past your pain. Don't allow your feelings to change the facts of who God made you to be.

Anything that is left unresolved will fester and continue to manifest itself until you do the work to heal. You have to be willing to dig deep into the painful places in order to heal. But if you do the work, healing will take place. I am a living witness that when you put in the work, transformation and healing will come. I found my strength, and I pray you find yours as well. I believe in you, but more importantly, I pray that you will believe in yourself.

My Padded Walls

Felicia Ellis

I remember the small, square room with the padded walls that I would be locked in for days. The colors, blue, green, and gray, are still vividly sketched in my mind and serve as a reminder of some of the darkest hours of my life. At the age of fifteen, a psychiatric facility in Richmond, Virginia would become my home for four agonizing months. I remember the day I heard the therapist say to my parents, "I would like to keep her here for observation over the weekend." I remember my cries falling on deaf ears as my parents nodded their heads in agreement. They would allow me to stay for the weekend. However, that weekend would last for months, causing severe damage to an already emotionally and physically scarred teenage girl.

Abuse should have served as my middle name. That was the life I knew from the age of seven to well into my adult life. My first encounter of abuse was sexual; I was molested by a trusted family friend. At the age of seven, I was aware that what the individual was doing to me was wrong, and was able to express that information to my parents. However, to my surprise, they did not believe me. According to them, I'd made it all up in my head. That individual was incapable of doing anything of that nature to a child; plus, he loved me as if I were one of his own. From that day forward, I would suffer in silence while all accusations against him would be swept under the rug, and I would be labeled a troubled child. As the abuse continued, I remained silent. It wasn't until I became a teenager that my life would begin to change—for the worse.

It was during my teenage years that I started smoking, drinking, and sneaking out of the house to hang out with friends and, sometimes, older men. I used them as a distraction to hide the hurt and pain that would lie dormant within me for many, many years. I had no other outlets and no one to run to or share my sorrows with. My actions were attributed to the hurtful words I would repeatedly hear from the mouths of my close family members, that I would never amount to anything, and this is truly what I began to believe. I was fearful, angry, and moving in the wrong direction. I became overly promiscuous, looking for love in all the wrong places. It was a love that I would never find because I equated love with sex. My abuser convinced me that love was all about sex. For the longest time, I could never figure out why I couldn't get any of the men I slept with to love me; after all, if I gave them what they wanted, it should equate to love, right? In my world, that's what I was taught to believe; the reality was that those men would never love me, only use my body for their pleasure for as long as I would allow it. Unfortunately, I would eventually learn the bitter truth and walk away many times with a broken heart.

It was also during my teenage years that I reached out for help. I thought reaching out to someone other than a family member would get me the help that I needed. However, they reached out in turn to one of my family members instead of going to the authorities or contacting social services. The family assured them that I was a liar and a very troubled girl, and shared my cry for help with my parents. This prompted them to get me the help they felt I needed. It was finally time for me to meet with a psychiatrist, and after just one session I had been diagnosed. I just sat there, listening to her going back and forth with my parents, and not once did she ask me my side of the story. My parents were convinced that they had found me help—or so they thought. But they only added fuel to an already blazing fire.

I was admitted to the facility, and this is the place I would experience my second episode of sexual abuse, this time by an eighteen-year-old female. The abuse would continue for about a month, and each time she would threaten to hurt me if I told anyone. I was afraid to tell anyone for fear of her hurting me, but I was also fearful that my cries of sexual abuse would again be totally ignored. I was unable to eat or sleep and became withdrawn from everyone in our unit. I refused to participate in my daily one-on-one therapy sessions, nor would I attend evening group sessions. The isolation led my psychiatrist to prescribe me three different types of medication that would calm me, but which also caused erratic behavior. One night, after my roommate finished having her way with me, I went into a raging fit that sent me reeling totally out of control. I was given a shot to calm me down, placed in a straitjacket, and hauled into the infamous padded room for the first time. This room would become my solace. It would also become my way of escape from my current abuser. If I continued to act crazy, I would be placed in the padded room. No one could hurt me in that space. I was scared and alone, but unharmed. Day after day I would sit like a ragdoll in the corner of the padded cell. I had no one to talk to—and I believe this is where I finally lost my voice, confidence, and will to live. I decided that I wanted to die, but had nothing I could use to end my life.

A few weeks into my stay, I had my first face-to-face meeting with my parents, which did not go well. I wanted to go home, but because of my raging fits they were told that I was too unstable and unpredictable to go home. Further treatment was needed. I tried to explain to my parents everything that I was going through in that place and tried to convince them that I did not belong there. Of course, they listened to the psychiatrist instead. I became hysterical, yelling and acting out in the presence of my parents. This gave the doctor the ammunition she needed to make sure my parents would continue to side with her, as they could see with their own eyes that I was unstable. Why couldn't they see my cry for help? Why were they unable to see my hurt and pain? Weren't they supposed to protect me? How could they leave me after I told them about my horrific experiences in that place? I would never receive those answers. That would be the last visit where they would hear my voice in any of our family sessions. I was mute. I sat in a chair in front of them each visit, staring at the walls. It was over; I was done with them. I felt like my parents had permanently stolen my voice.

The medications had me in a daze; I was numb to feelings and most of my days were spent sleeping. I was so out of it that I didn't know the time of day, nor was I aware of the days of the week. I was totally disconnected from everything and everyone around me. But one day an angel by the name of Ms. Ana came into my life. She was new to the staff and would become the first person to show me love and give me hope. She also believed my story. Ms. Ana bought me a small Bible and would pray with me every day, reminding me of God's constant love and devotion to His children. She also taught me how to channel my energy by journaling. It wasn't long thereafter that I was returned to the normal living unit. Ms. Ana made sure I had a new roommate and wrote a report of the reoccurring abuse I had endured with my last roommate. Though I started attending group therapy again, I was not yet ready to continue my one-on-one sessions with my psychiatrist or with my parents. In the end, I would never get the opportunity to converse with them again in that particular setting, as my insurance ran out and I was sent to another mental facility in Petersburg, Virginia.

It was at the new mental facility that I would meet another angel: my new psychiatrist, Dr. Richardson. Within a few days I was taken off all medications. He would spend an hour a day with me for weeks, reprogramming and coaching me back to a healthy state. I was allowed no visits with my parents until he was sure I could face them without regressing. Finally, I was ready to stand my ground and not allow them or anyone else to convince me that I was crazy. I was a victim of abuse who needed help coping with the trauma I had experienced. Though I was scared to face my parents, I knew that if I didn't, I would never free myself from the bondage of mental institutions. A month later, I sat across from my parents and listened to my angel, Dr. Richardson, say that "there is and never was anything wrong with this child." He told them, "She never needed medication and has been off of it for over a month." He explained to them that he believed my story and that all I needed was a regular therapist to help me deal with my abuse issues. I was sent home by the end of the week, and would continue to see Dr. Richardson at his outpatient facility for three years, prescription-free.

During my adult years I accepted Christ as my Savior, and my dependency on Him would be my support through all obstacles. However, along my adult journey I would face two rapes and domestic abuse. These incidents set me back and returned me to a dark place that I could never imagine. Though I sought help and prayed, the pain was overwhelming, and I attempted suicide several times. I started drinking, smoking, and popping pills. It didn't matter the type of pills,

I would take them. For weeks I would drink until I could no longer stand, take a bottle of pills, and pray I wouldn't wake up in the morning. I always woke up and became angry with God because He would not allow me to die. I was unable to function in my day-to-day life, and things became so unbearable that I had a nervous breakdown. I locked myself in my house and cried out to God day after day and night after night. I knew He could put all the scattered pieces of my life together and make them whole again, I just didn't know how. Deep within, I felt that God wanted something from me and I was determined to find out what that was. There was no way He would allow me to go through so much pain for no purpose.

One night, God spoke clearly to me, giving me a scripture, Philippians 4:3. It says, "And I entreat thee also, true yokefellow, help those women which labored with me in the gospel, with Clement also, and with other my fellow laborers, whose names are in the book of life." The key words that hit me like a ton of bricks were "help those women." My pain was to be used for His glory. Years later, God would give me the name of my ministry: HerHealing. But at the time, because of my hurt, pain, and insecurities, I felt like I wasn't capable of helping others. I was ruined in so many ways. I felt dirty and nasty. I was still broken, and though I heard the voice of the Lord, I decided that I was not worthy of living out the purpose He had planned for my life. It wasn't until six years later, after I worked hard to rebuild my self-worth, that my ministry was launched.

Everyone is capable of covering up their pain and insecurities. I was a professional at it, and able to do it for many years. I had a great job, nice car, designer bags and shoes, nice clothes, and my own home. These are the things that I used to falsify my happiness. These are things that I would use to convince those on the outside looking in that I had it going on. I was that girl. But I was also that girl who would curl up in a ball every night in her bed and cry herself to sleep. I was also that girl that smoked and drank to dull the pain of my demons just to get a good night's rest.

Today, I'm not perfect. But I am an overcomer. I am strong and determined to live my life, even though it has been altered and has deterred me for many years. My demons still rear their heads, but I have the power within me to not allow them to defeat me. They can no longer hurt or hinder me. I accept the fact that I am a beautiful flower with a few missing petals, and that even so I am still whole. I accept the little girl, teenager, and woman that was sexually and physically abused; they are parts of me that helped shape who I am today. I accept that I will never be able to tell a story of having a normal childhood. I accept that my life is different than some and very similar to others. I have accepted my calling and God's plan for my life to help other women.

There are many tools to help overcome your hurts and pains. Prayer, counseling, and the help of friends can aid you. I used all of these, and also incorporated my experiences by acknowledging my story, being determined to change my story, and standing tall and bold enough to finally tell my story to help others. I regret nothing and appreciate the love that God has for me in choosing and trusting me to be a testimony.

Loving yourself and knowing who and whose you are plays a very important role in your ability to heal. The impossible is possible and the unforgivable is forgivable. My story is not me, but it is about me. My prayer is that my story will motivate my sisters who feel they are unable to find a way out of their own padded walls. Each of our padded rooms holds different stories, but no matter the story, there is a way out.

Prescription for the abscess of abuse

Embrace your padded walls and the discomfort that comes with them. It is a part of you and will aid in the development of the woman you are becoming. Use your scars as an agent for change. No one wants to stay stuck in the same place; it causes too much agony and leaves you stagnant in your growth. Lastly, share your story to help someone else, as I just did!

Hurts, Habits, Hang-Ups, and Emotional Heredity

Removing the Face of Counterfeit Wellness

Charleta D. M. Harvey, MAML

This is a story of unresolved trauma, isolation, and superhero syndrome. I grew up in a home where domestic violence was an issue; happy times were rare—fussing and fighting were more of the "norm." By the time I was eight, my parents—well, at least my mom—had called it quits, and she began the process of leaving my dad. As part of the transition, I began living at my great-grandmother's house. One thing that became an unfortunate part of that transition was the fact that my "innocence" was misappropriated, subsequently robbing me of my ability to simply remain a little girl because the misappropriation taught me things I shouldn't have known at such an age.

Misappropriation of my innocence taught me how bodily violations don't always seem real—either because of emotional manipulation, or because you don't realize until you (maybe) hear it spoken of out loud, and once you hear something, you can't un-hear it. In my case, I overheard my abuser speak openly about his treatment of me. This ceased his behavior when he didn't get approval from the friend in whom he confided the secret. But my overhearing this conversation immediately taught me that all that had happened was . . . WRONG. Bad. A secret never to be shared. And thus, because I was also taught that my truth would devastate others, and it wasn't "right" to hurt *them* . . . I became a master of people pleasing. I learned in the most extreme ways to ignore my feelings . . . to push them down, away, or otherwise render them nonexistent, because apparently how I felt didn't matter. I learned to lie by omission, not realizing that in doing so, I would cause myself years of anguish, while also being initiated into a group whose membership no person—especially a child—should have . . . sexual abuse survivor.

Being relegated to the "secret keeper society," I also eventually developed a survivalist mentality, a habit which saw me attempt to prove my "worth" in other ways, namely academics, at least in the early years. I became the child who excelled at everything; I won countless awards throughout grade school and achieved still more in tandem with those awards. I was the goody-goody, the one on whom my family could depend to achieve and "do well" . . . and so I did, time and again. I was simultaneously both unfazed and haunted by all of the hell happening around me—including an extremely fractured "relationship" with my father, who was no longer a regular part of my daily life.

Somewhere in my mid-teens, I began to crave an escape from the goody-goody persona, so I found ways to "safely" rebel. Growing up in the inner city, there was always something happening or someone dying; because of this, there was also room for lots of attention from the dope boys. This became my outlet, Little Miss Goody-Goody giving the dope boys the time of day, not because I should've, but just because I could. Too young and immature to care, I actually "dated" a couple of them—if you can call it that, since sitting on your front porch talking to or flirting with a drug dealer isn't really dating . . . Still, I very much enjoyed the attention. But what if, in a moment of conversation, someone decided it was time for that dude (the dope boy) to die and I got caught in the crossfire?! That actually happened a few times, and I came THIS CLOSE to becoming a casualty in someone else's war. But, God. Enough about that, back to "doing well."

By the time I'd reached high school, I was an academic rock star, earning high marks and well on the way to getting my ticket out of the ghetto punched. Destination: bigger and better things. The very first college I got accepted to, I attended. I was on "do well" autopilot . . . until I wasn't. Not too far into freshman year, I began to crash and burn. I wasn't happy with my direction in school. There were challenges and pressures both in my college environment and at home, and it all got to be too much. Initially too proud to fail and too ashamed to ask for help, I mentally checked out from pretty much everything, sitting in class but not being "present," yet keeping up the facade that I was "in it to win it" and doing well. Soon enough, my house of cards was to come tumbling down.

I fluctuated between indifference and confusion: indifference because I'd "checked out," confusion because I wasn't completely sure what was happening, why it was happening, or how (or even if) I could stop it from happening. After all, I was the goody-goody known for doing well. Um, not so much anymore . . . I vacillated between extreme depression and something I call *counterfeit wellness*. And you know what? These two states of being simply cannot coexist! So, remember that "house of cards"? It eventually came crashing down, and brought with it an inevitable reality check that I should've expected, but still wasn't quite prepared for . . . I was flunking out of school. One more problem to add to an already overloaded list of disappointments and shame, a.k.a. my hurts, habits, and hang-ups. And let me tell you, shame is a powerful tool of distraction and mental oppression, so much so that I soon found myself wondering, "how in the world did I let this happen?" and "what in the world am I gonna do about it?" They say that you do better when you know better. Well, I definitely "knew" better, but couldn't seem to manage how to "do" better. And yet, in the eyes of my family, for all intents and purposes, I was doing just fine.

There are absolutely no coincidences. When I think back to that time, I realize that a "chance" meeting is what landed me on a therapist's couch, right where I needed to be. As I began pouring out my heart, frustrated and ashamed by my shortcomings and lack of successes, something extraordinary happened. Up until the time that I began therapy, I had always believed that my "issue" was my inability to figure out my path, and that that was impacting my ability to chart the course of my future. But what was eventually revealed was that the insufficiency I felt was a result of my daddy issues. Didn't for a second see that one coming! My home was "broken" long before the actual "break" happened, and from that chasm emanated all kinds of abuse and physical and emotional trauma, all kinds of hurt, that had lasting effects long before the "effects" were actually realized. And through all of that, my daddy was (mostly) nowhere to be found. Internally, I was wondering, "How could he leave, check out? Wasn't I enough to make him stay?" Apparently, not so much. The revelation: I had a "father," but needed a "dad."

Through regularly going to therapy, I began to deal with my issues, but didn't necessarily feel any better about my capacity to resolve them. In fact, at least in the beginning, what I mostly remember is feeling more disappointment and shame in myself, adding to my hang-ups. Plus, though she was well-intentioned, looking back I don't really think that the college campus therapist was equipped to deal with the full scope of my challenges, so that only made experiencing the matter worse. Eventually, our time together fizzled out rather than ended. At that point, I guessed I was supposed to have been "cured" and able to cope. Sure. Okay. Whatever . . . enter more counterfeit wellness.

On the bright side of things, I was no longer flunking out of school, but not because I'd started making any effort to improve. To the contrary, since I was dealing with an issue of emotional wellness (or lack thereof) that was obviously impacting my studies, I was given the opportunity to medically withdraw from classes with virtually no impact on my overall standing in school. This medical withdrawal allowed me to hide in plain sight . . . no one at school had a clue that I was no longer a student; and my family? Well, they were even more clueless. Beyond the passive, standardized inquiries like "how's school going?" and my usual (strategically enthusiastic) response of "great," no one ever really checked on me. In the African-American community, at least at the time, no one, especially in my family, really talked about their feelings in healthy ways. This is one of the reasons why, in some regards and in my opinion, we as a people remain tethered to mental shackles.

Remember, I was the one expected to do well. I was the one who didn't need help because I had it all together. However, I was the one in real trouble! Existing in this way has a double-edged sword of consequence: although I needed it, I didn't get real help and support from my family because I didn't ask for it; I didn't ask for the help and support from them because they believed I was the one least in need of it.

So, I suffered, perpetuating madness. Time passes, as it does, and though I would return to school for a time, I eventually left for good, taking my mediocre grades and emotional baggage with me. One thing I also took with me was the possibility of a new, healthy relationship. By way of another chance encounter, I'd met a guy from the Midwest . . . very handsome, well-mannered, and intelligent. Little did I know, this relationship too would come with a new set of emotional baggage. Here. I. Go. Again.

I honestly don't know what's worse . . . having family experiences that diminish you as a person and leave you feeling inadequate, or being dismissed as inadequate by those who will also one day become "family" before they even really get to know you. The benefit of the doubt is real, necessary, and important; when you don't get the benefit of the doubt through no fault of your own, it can be devastating. My humble, seemingly unpolished roots and heritage of familial divorce were far too much for my (now) husband's family, and because that seed of people-pleasing had been planted long ago, I spent far too much time, even before we were married, needing to be where I wasn't wanted . . . once again trying to prove my worth. This opened the door to many an argument, caused turmoil between my husband and his parents, and led to a kind of coexistent tolerance that teemed with isolation . . . *because he chose me.*

As we started a family, skeletons from the past emerged and threatened to destroy everything. A moment of shared intimacy unintentionally took me back to my sexual violation as a child and thrust me into a place I struggled to fight my way out of as I grieved the child I never got to be. The revelation of my violation was too much for my husband, and he too struggled; he struggled to help me through depression, struggled to understand how I could've kept such a secret from him; struggled to understand the emotional anatomy of a sexual abuse survivor. There were real wounds that needed to be cleaned up so they could properly heal, but instead we put Band-Aids on them and went about life.

After a few years, we had another child. My husband's military career continued to propel onward and upward. More responsibility. More expectations—unrealistic and otherwise. More time apart in service to our country. We experienced incredible highs and lows during our time together, but the stressors of life eventually became too much, and despite our best efforts the marriage shattered into a million pieces. Rebuilding after such devastation is difficult even in the best of relational circumstances; it is all the more difficult when you are physically together, but emotionally a million miles apart. I never understood the idea of being lonely in your marriage until it happened to me. I will be the first to say that I seriously entertained divorce, but God was very clear in showing me that I had not yet been released from my marriage. So, I had to figure out how to "stay" and grow through the challenges. A dear sister-friend advised me: "Love your husband and trust God."

Being in the midst of it, there were many days when I found that difficult . . . both my head and heart were no longer in it. I loved him as the father of my children, but honestly, nothing more. Unhealed wounds inflicted on both sides because of the baggage we each brought to the relationship, distance and time to reflect on *the distance*, and communication challenges were all brought to bear. Through the ups and downs of life, I had experienced a lot of trauma, and this trauma was informing my life's stagnant existence, rather than being the circumstances by which I drew on the strength within me to thrive instead of just survive. This was a time when I needed God like never before. So, to first get healing for myself and then work on healing my marriage, I really had to lean in. Faith had to take me places that dwelling on past failures could not. Through counseling and a focused effort toward improving my covenant relationship with God, things began to change. But, in order for measurable change to happen, I had to first acknowledge and accept that change was absolutely necessary.

An element of this was the recognition that sometimes things happen *for* me, and not *to* me. In order to be free of counterfeit wellness, I had to choose the best parts of myself as sources of love, and the least, most un-liked parts of myself as the areas where I would learn to develop self-acceptance in my quest to become "whole." Before I could admire anyone else, I had to admire my own tenacity in the face of adversity. I had to show myself genuine compassion and be mindful of the mental shifts necessary for my transformation. I had to become my own She-ro, deciding to love myself first . . . by any means necessary.

Prescription for the chronic pain of counterfeit wellness

Trauma of any kind causes emotional pain that interferes with the ability to live the life desired instead of the one settled for. Triage the situation and acknowledge that the pain, however deep, exists. Then, the first steps to treatment must be an honest evaluation of the obstacles to and assets for healing—people, thoughts, and behaviors. Take two pieces of paper. On one, list your "assets" for healing, naming the people who uplift and inspire you, as well as your thought patterns and behaviors that genuinely help you to be your best self. On the other, list the "obstacles"—people who represent toxic relationships (even if they happen to be family), as well as your current thought patterns and behaviors that are self-defeating. Next, evaluate and gather the necessary resources to eliminate your obstacles as you increase your assets. Put in the time to do the work, however long it takes. Repeat the treatment as necessary, showing yourself unending compassion in the process.

Growing Through the Challenges of "I'll Be Happy When..."

Laura C. Bembry

When I was younger, I told myself that once I got married, I would be happy. I would have more money and more fun, and would be able to travel like I hadn't been able to do while I was single. At the beginning of my twelve years of marriage, I never would have thought things would be as they are today. Yet, at forty-five years of age, I found myself divorced and navigating through this journey called life once again by myself. This didn't feel like happiness to me.

During the process of separation, I spent a lot of time placing the blame elsewhere and asking myself several questions. Would I have been happy in my marriage if money weren't an issue? Would we still be together or even married if we would have dated longer? What if I had made more sacrifices? It was also during this time that I began to have deeper moments of reflection and inspection of myself, ones that I had not previously had. I started to focus on me, my actions, and how I played a role in the destruction of my marriage. It was a level of self-inspection I had not taken the time to do before.

I once read a quote from actor Will Smith. He was talking about his wife and how they had come to a realization about happiness. He said that what they had concluded was that "her happiness was her responsibility and my happiness was my responsibility . . . It's unfair and it's kind of unrealistic and can be destructive to place responsibility for your happiness on anybody other than yourself." His statement hit me like a ton of bricks as I thought about how my actions played a major role in the collapse of my marriage. I realized that I had made my happiness contingent upon things I expected my ex-husband to do, without having communicated to him what those things were. It wasn't until then that I was able to admit that I had expected him to complete me, instead of him complementing me. I discovered that in areas of my life where I didn't want to put in the work, I wanted him to fill those gaps, thus creating happiness for me—or so I thought. Recognizing this was huge for me. I realized through my self-inspection that I had placed limitations on what I could accomplish as an individual. I had to face myself and the things I had been hiding about myself for years. I was ready to remove the face of feeling like a fraud. I had been performing in front of others as if I was whole, but I was really feeling broken on the inside. It was time to do the work. It was time for me to go back and figure out where my brokenness began and why I was living in a constant state of "I'll be happy when . . ."

Growing up, my father would always tell me that two people working together is better than what one person can do alone. He was speaking from his experiences and the challenges he had faced. When I found it challenging to work toward having those things in life that I thought equated to happiness, I felt disadvantaged. I felt as if I needed someone to compensate for what I lacked in order to achieve those things. I decided, maybe it was just one of those things that I needed someone else to help me achieve. After all, two people working together are better than one, right?

As I moved into my mid-twenties, I began to realize that finances were a challenge for me. I knew I needed to do something because I had racked up a substantial amount of debt at a young age. So, I decided to seek help from a credit counseling agency. With their help and my determination, I actually managed to become debt free. I was so happy with myself that I was able to accomplish something by digging myself out of debt. However, that was only the beginning. In years to come, I would repeatedly go through the same cycle of racking up debt, repaying it, then racking up more debt again. At that time, I had decided in my mind that I could not be successful at managing money, and that when I got married, it would be to someone who was financially savvy.

When I finally met my husband, he was just that. He was financially savvy AND he was an accountant. I thought that this would resolve all my brokenness surrounding my inability to manage my finances successfully. He met all the criteria that was on my list of what I wanted in a husband. We had a short courtship, and during that time, it would appear to anyone looking from the outside-in that I was put together well financially. My sister and I owned a townhome together, and I drove a very nice vehicle and had a good paying job. My career was moving upward and things looked great from the outside. If I would have removed the face of being a fraud with my finances then, it could have given him an opportunity to assess whether or not those things were deal-breakers for him. It would have at least given him greater insight into what he was going to have to deal with. But instead I made him responsible for my happiness. I'll be happy when . . .

I wanted the finer things in life but didn't address the fact that I had poor management skills. I knew I wasn't good at it, but hadn't put in the work necessary to really address my long-standing problems with money. I was a hustler when it came to my budget, with no historical reference on how to properly manage money. My immediate family was also poor at managing money, perfecting the art of robbing Peter to pay Paul. That alone should have alerted me that I needed to gain more knowledge and would have to work at this thing, but it didn't. Needless to say, my now-ex and I fought about money constantly. He was the saver and I was the free spirit in the relationship. He was great with money and strategic with saving and investing. I, on the other hand, always had to be reined in while he struggled to keep our finances in check so we could save for our future and have all those other things we wanted in life. I fully understood the goals we had agreed upon and the benefits of sticking with the budget, but that still didn't stop me from challenging the plan quite often. And, in the midst of our other problems, I would often use spending to comfort myself and would rebel against the budget he so diligently worked to build.

I give this experience as an example of something I expected my ex to resolve in order for me to be happy. I placed the responsibility for my happiness in his hands when I should have taken responsibility for myself. I hadn't put in the work to overcome this struggle. He had no idea that I had placed this unfair expectation upon him without even discussing it with him. All he knew was that I was unhappy, and he didn't quite understand why. On the surface, I appeared to be someone who was a good steward over my money. But this was not the case. And so, I made my happiness contingent upon him fixing my financial struggles. This problem didn't surface until after we were married. As a result, we fought often about our finances, and I was unhappy. I was delusional to expect that either he or more money could fix the problem. And as you can expect, due to my spending, we weren't able to travel like I had anticipated, which further contributed to my unhappiness. But in actuality, I could have traveled more when I was single if I had been better at saving money.

This issue, although major, wasn't the sole cause of the end of our marriage, but it made me more keenly aware of the role I played toward that end. Oftentimes, we bring the baggage of "I'll be happy when" into our lives or marriages without even realizing it. For some of us, if we've identified this as something we struggle with, we can work at overcoming this particular challenge. Awareness is the first step to healing. I encourage you not just to move on from it, but to also heal from it. These are what I like to call growth moments, when we choose to learn from situations we may not like; it's a *learn*, not a *like*. The very first time I became debt free, I had paid the bills off, but didn't address the overall dysfunction of living beyond my means. As a result, I went through the same cycle, over and over again. I had moved on from it, but I had not healed from it.

My goal is to provide you with four categories of thoughts to ponder over that can help you grow through moments of "I'll be happy when . . ." These can assist you to begin making steps toward understanding what happiness really means to you and acknowledging those things that may be hindering you from experiencing it. The goal is for you to be able to experience happiness wherever you are in life. These are things that have helped me in my journey of growing through "I'll be happy when . . ."

Sometimes it's hard to pinpoint a deeply rooted issue, something that may have been ingrained in you due to how you grew up, or because of an experience, or even because of a specific season in your life. At times, things come to light through surface situations or experiences, meaning on the surface it appears to be something simple, but as we dig deeper, we realize it's tied to something more complex.

The following questions will help you gain greater insight into your feelings and actions as a result of situations that may occur or may have already happened in the past.

Discovery

When faced with an opportunity for self-discovery, ask yourself the following questions:

- Why did it impact me?
- How did it impact me?
- Did it resurface past hurts? Is there a common denominator?
- Does it have the possibility of affecting me long-term?
- How can I position my mind, body, and soul so it won't hinder my growth?

Reflection

When faced with an opportunity for self-reflection, ask yourself the following questions:

- Did I play a role in it?

- Did I exercise emotional intelligence? Remember, emotional intelligence—the capacity to be aware of, control, and express one's emotions, and to handle interpersonal relationships judiciously and empathetically—is not a gift, it's a choice.

- Was this a growth moment? Meaning, was there something to learn from this experience?

- Is there any repair I need to do? Some possibilities may be needing to apologize, admit wrongdoing, or speak your truth (it's not what you say, it's how you say it). What you may need to do in order to repair may be beyond this list; however, the goal is to acknowledge and perform the necessary repair needed to be able to move forward in a healthy manner.

Inspection

When faced with an opportunity for self-inspection, ask yourself the following questions:

- What was your motive or intention? Be honest.

- What are you focused on? Learn to manage your thoughts; thoughts and feelings have power that can help or hurt you.

- What can YOU do to improve your situation, instead of waiting for someone else to come and "save" you?

- Have you put in the work? Be honest!

Positive Outlets

Don't just move on from it, heal from it. Life can be a battlefield. Every day we need to rejuvenate. What's your rejuvenation process? How do you maintain the health of your mind, body, and soul? Possibilities might include:

- Working out
- Eating well
- Meditation
- Gardening
- Reading
- Sleeping (a healthy amount)
- Reading scripture

This is just a small list of activities that can help rejuvenate you from the challenges of life. The goal is to ensure that whatever you choose as your positive outlet, it is healthy and beneficial to your mind, body, and soul.

After separating from my husband, I was able to rebuild my life and become better at managing my finances. Am I perfect at managing my finances? No, but I have taken classes, read books, and watched videos to help strengthen this area of weakness in my life. As a result, I was able to purchase a brand-new home all on my own, one of the largest homes

I've ever lived in. Ain't God good! God isn't looking for you to be perfect, but simply to make progress. You see, it was in me all the time! And it's also within you! I just had to be honest with myself about my actions and the reasoning behind my actions. I was my own worst enemy and had confined myself within fictitious walls of limitation. Don't get me wrong, I do believe there are times when God places people in our lives to help lift us up. But we shouldn't expect someone else to be responsible for making us happy. Happiness shouldn't be based upon how another person can compensate for what you lack. We limit our happiness when we choose to put the work of our own healing into someone else's hands. This places unfair expectations on the other person without them even being aware. We owe it to ourselves to look deeper and gain great insight into our feelings and actions.

Life is a journey, and things may not happen in the order you thought they would occur. We may have to take a different path or repeat some lessons, but it's all a part of the work you put into owning your happiness and striving for progress on a daily basis; not perfection, progress. Learn to celebrate the wins in your life versus being focused on the losses.

It's also important to know that your journey is unique, as is God's plan and purpose for your life. Don't compare your journey to someone else's, for it will only steal your joy. Be mindful of what you allow your mind to focus on and how it makes you feel. If your focus leads you to a depressive, dark state, this is a red flag that you need to change your focus. Many of us struggle with seeing others' success and use it as a gauge of where we are in our lives. However, is what we're comparing ourselves to even valid or true? In the age of social media, you tend to only see who people "post" to be, and not who they really are. Your comparison is then based upon something fictional created in the eye of the beholder.

Prescription for the infection of fraudulent happiness

Instead of focusing on what you lack, what you haven't done, or what you may still be battling with, focus on what you have accomplished and where you are today. Sit down and think about what happiness actually means to you in your current season of life. What you see as happiness can evolve, and it's important to reassess what it means to you in the moment. What you previously thought would make you happy may no longer be an accurate marker. Learn to find joy in the life you're living. And although you may experience thoughts of "I'll be happy when . . ." from time to time, the goal is to recognize the feeling and call it out. Make a choice not to dwell on or linger in those moments, but to instead use the tidbits I've provided to guide you through that self-inspection and reflection that is needed so that you can own and grasp your happiness in the moment.

Removing the Face of the Unbearable

Jackie Togun

Unbearable. It used to be the best way to describe my current workplace experience. After interviewing for the position, I accepted the job offer with joy and anticipation. Little did I know that I was beginning what would become one of the most unbearable job experiences of my life. From day to day, as I clocked in, I began to see disorganization in the flow of the workday, lack of communication amongst team members, and an absence of quality care being given to those being served by the organization. These conditions were so profound and detailed that I became distressed, frustrated, and angry. My desire at that point was to make my exit.

You see, I have a history of "running" when situations become unbearable. But because I have grown to value God's plans for me, I paused to gather my thoughts and my emotions. Was I supposed to exit or was I supposed to stay? In order to feel that I was doing everything I could to hear God clearly, I increased my time of fasting and prayer. I also started another job search. Meanwhile, I believed it was important to make the best of what I deemed to be a bad situation. I began to look at my circumstance from a different perspective. I attached "purpose" to my dilemma. I reflected on how I ended up with the job in the first place.

I decided that, until I truly had clarity about my going or staying, I needed to change my attitude, or should I say my "emotiontude." I pulled together some survival strategies that I believed would help me to "work through" the pain of this workplace. First, I took a closer look at my situation through the lens of purpose. It was there that I found ways to effectively and productively cope, such as being able to pray for those around me and being a witness to the day-to-day workplace happenings and personal transformations. Next, I internally created a new title for my position, based on my purpose. It was my secret. I also gave my workplace a different name, based on what was really happening on a daily basis, instead of what was supposed to be happening on a daily basis. This was also my secret. I then started to prioritize my job tasks in a different way. Each day, I would decide what battles to fight and what battles to refrain from fighting. I also resorted to a consistent soft or quiet response to each situation that had to be resolved.

I had to forgive some people that I worked with. Without my consciously realizing it, I had built up resentment and bitterness toward persons in leadership positions. I was frustrated about how they were leading, their lack of concern for the people around them, and how they were interacting. Before I knew it, their very presence triggered an anger in me that disturbed my very consciousness. When I realized what was happening, I talked to God about how I was feeling and asked Him to forgive me. I released the feelings of unforgiveness toward leadership in general. With one particular leader, I bought a gift and card and made sure that it was put in her mailbox. This was a real sacrifice for me, as at that particular time, I only had $4.00 to spare. It was spent on her gift and her card.

I became extremely sensitive to what I would say via conversations and who I would converse with. I would not allow myself to be a part of negative talk or gossip. I would deliberately promote conversations that were positive whenever possible and I would remain neutral or quiet around negativity whenever I could. At home, I started going to bed earlier. I changed my eating habits, including times to eat and what types of foods to eat. I also became more aggressive about blocking out relaxation time, with deliberate activities that would allow me to just have some fun!

Some days, the highway on the way to work looked splattered because of the tears that covered my face. Other days, I clocked out, sat in my car, took a deep breath, and cried softly until I had to go wherever it was that I was going. There were also days when I cried both going to work and coming home, all in the same day. On one occasion, I spent most of the weekend in the hospital due to "stroke precautions." However, I am convinced that that weekend served many purposes as it pertains to bearing the unbearable. While in the hospital with IVs running in my arms, taking all sorts of tests and having doctors, nurses, and technicians coming in and out of my room, I was forced to examine how I was living my life—and how life was living me! I questioned how well I was loving, nurturing, and protecting myself. The bigger question looming in the back of my mind was why now, why this way? I am grateful that all the tests were negative and that I'm still able to be part of a team in a workplace.

As I look back over the past couple of years, I take no credit for being able to bear the pain of an unbearable workplace. There are some ever-present truths about who God is and how He does what He does that have kept me steadfast. God is sovereign. This truth in and of itself is paramount, foundational, and ultimate. It is a cushion and a safety net that keeps us from falling and crumbling, because we know how much He loves us. The very essence of His right to reign in us affirms that He really does have the last word in our lives. And so, if we can embrace His authority, we can accept the truth that His purpose, His plan, and His perfecting is unfailing.

Purpose reminds us that God created each of us for His glory. Because we are made in His image and likeness, we're not just haphazardly existing. We are here on this earth at a specific time and for a specific reason. It is important that we love God enough and ourselves enough that we take the time to find out what our purpose is. Spending time with God through praise, worship, prayer, study of His Word, fellowship, giving, fasting, and serving are all ways that can help bring clarity to our purpose. There is also no substitute for getting to know yourself, who you are mentally, physically, emotionally, and socially. This knowledge of self causes an appreciation that fosters the fullness of who we are spiritually, as well as what we've been sent here on earth to do.

God's plan helps us to know that God has not left us without a way to fulfill His purpose for us, even when sometimes we go left when God has said "go right." It is wisdom on our part to want to know the plan of God for our lives. We would save ourselves a lot of time, energy, effort, money, and distress if we learned to be a willing part of the way that God wants our purpose to be walked out on a daily basis. His goal for us is to ultimately come out as the "winner," to be that one that He can "brag" about. Knowing this about God, that He really is our main cheerleader, is life-changing and mindboggling!

God's perfecting of us challenges us to trust Him with our very lives. This is where bearing the unbearable can get tough. We can't be a reflection of God's eyes, feet, hands, voice, and heart if we don't surrender ourselves to the process of being able to show His nature to the world. Because our sinful nature does not readily reflect God's nature, we have to change. Through God's love for us, He nurtures us, teaches us, tests us, prunes us, and stretches us. These moments and seasons don't all come in the same way or at the same time.

Often, it is because of who we are and where we are in our own process that the circumstances we face become unbearable. What we experience in life will be personal to what we need from life. And many times what we need in life is not just for us, but also for some of the lives that we will meet along our journey.

The light at the end of the tunnel is that God is molding and shaping us into the person that He has always planned for us to be. This understanding can be a part of what propels us into our destiny. And so, when we face the unbearable, we can reflect on who God is. He is sovereign. His nature is to love and care for that which He has created. He is our main cheerleader! We can remember that because we belong to Him, we have purpose, and that God's purpose is going to happen. We can remember all of the times that God has already delivered us, as well as the situations that He has already brought us through. And finally, we can know that we have all that we need to bear the unbearable. This is a certainty that can only come and stay if we have made a conscious decision to live this life, this journey that we call life, God's way. It is through His way that we have His promises, His provisions, and His protection. Within these dynamics of a God-lived life, we are able to have peace and rest. We can believe when we can't see our way. We can trust when we want to be afraid. We experience strength that we know we didn't give to ourselves. We receive grace and mercy that we know we don't deserve. We have hope that gives us assurance that everything is going to be all right.

So, I stayed in this workplace. Being able to smile, not expecting what should be expected, and letting go of unforgiveness have all been made possible because I made a conscious decision to behave God's way in the workplace. My choices have not gone unrewarded. On a daily basis, most of my coworkers extend to me "good morning" gestures and "have a good evening" sentiments. Many in the community that I serve are quick to give me a smile, wave, or hug when they see me. A few of my coworkers make up a TLC Team. They are the ones that make sure I eat when a special event is in progress and food is available. There are others that, if I need something and they can get it, they make it happen. And then, there are a couple of "dear to my heart" people that I know I can count on; we talk, we pray, and we encourage one another in a very special way. God has also given me favor when it comes to technology. Because I'm not savvy in this area yet, it's always a blessing when someone comes to my rescue. Just recently, I received an unexpected "We love you" expression from some of my team members. I responded with thanks, but even now they don't know how much it means to me to have experienced their care.

Purpose is what I believe I have walked in thus far in this workplace. What started out as an unbearable situation actually gave way to an opportunity to serve others through prayer. In the hymn "What a Friend We Have in Jesus," there is this line: "What a privilege to carry everything to God in prayer." Because I have been able to cry out to God on behalf of this community, I have hope for the future of its people and I am encouraged concerning the outcome of the circumstances that they are enduring. I believe and know that, at the appointed time, God is going to fix what needs to be fixed. He always does! The icing on the cake is the fact that my life has changed forever. I now know that on the other side of unbearable are new blessings, new strength, and new understanding. And the glory all belongs to God!

Prescription for the ulcers from the unbearable

Hang up your runnin' shoes! Whatever your unbearable looks like, render that face powerless through changing your perspective, by redefining your circumstance, implementing the strategies that you have acquired, and taking time to give God the glory every step of the way!

The Public Figure's Mask, Exit Stage Left

Monique A. J. Smith

My story is similar to the movie *Rocketman*, the biopic of the rock star and public figure Elton John. He was famous for putting on elaborate costumes when he performed or made public appearances. But after the show, Elton John would engage in all types of activities to numb his feelings of being unsupported, unloved, unpopular, helpless, and hopeless. I too would wear elaborate dresses when serving as athletic administrator at athletic events, looking as if I had it all together. My story is not as drastic as the music superstar's, but the "masking" is the same for any public figure. The world's eyes never know the price that is paid.

This chapter is written for women in leadership or high-profile positions that wear the public-figure mask in their industry, but who are crying inside because of feelings akin to being misunderstood, overwhelmed, or viewed as imposters.

If you take off the mask periodically, if you set boundaries and communicate them, and if you do the work mentally, you can get better and not be bitter. Being bitter will hold you back personally and professionally. What does bitter look like? Like you can't be corrected. You would prefer to work in solitude than work with the team because you don't want to be criticized. You bite first to avoid having to interact or be bitten. And you do the same at home. At the time, you don't realize you are doing it; you just know you are about your business. Yet you wonder why you are not advancing.

So, why uncover the challenges of wearing a public figure's mask?

1. Unmasking is a healing process to live a full life.

2. The Bible says the truth will set you free—in this case, free of negative self-talk.

3. I want to be a help to others who follow in my footsteps.

4. My motto is "Planting Seeds of Empowerment to Lead Others to Greatness."

My story begins with a sense of being overwhelmed and trying to please everyone, even people I did not know. I represented progress in athletics for women in the early nineties due to my position as an interim athletics director at a small institution in Virginia, one of only a few women at the time to have such a position. But, just when the interim status was removed, I resigned and left the area, the position, and the institution.

Let me back up and tell you how I rose to be athletic director. I began in athletics as a public relations intern for an athletic conference office with three other mass media college students, all male. This gender dynamic became a trend. In the summer of 1987, I interned with BET—the only female among two other male college students. Then, at my first full-time job, I was blessed to work for the first female athletic director in that League, but I was still the only female sports information director in the league. My supervisor was a great example, but sadly, after I spent ten months being mentored by her, she was diagnosed with cancer and left the day-to-day operations of the office. After a year, she died. I was devastated. I was confused. I was grieving and in unfamiliar territory, having never before had anyone close to me die. That was the first time I *should* have sought counseling.

I remember her charge to me: "take care of my girls," the ballplayers she had coached and recruited. So I got to work and learned under fire how to be an administrator in athletics in all facets: financial aid, academic eligibility, student affairs, judicial affairs, account payments, scheduling—everything to support the girls. The responsibility was a welcomed pressure to honor her name and represent everything she stood for, because I couldn't let her down.

I was learning how to minister in athletics while still in my twenties, having outlasted five supervisors. I moved up the rankings both regionally and nationally, until I gained the opportunity to be a press steward for the Olympic Festival in 1995 and then for the Atlanta Olympics in 1996.

While at the Olympics, I received a call from the president of my institution, offering the athletic director's position on an interim basis. I hesitated and said "let me think about it." My concern was that I was a twenty-eight-year-old female with a marriage that was dissolving, and I didn't want to stay at the institution. Because my personal life was chipping away at my self-esteem, I didn't think I was ready to be athletic director, even though I was already functioning in the role. I decided I would call back the next day to decline.

That night the bomb exploded at the Olympic Park. As a result, I said that "life is short; I will take the position and learn on the job, like men do all the time." So there I was, at the mountaintop of my career, wearing the mask of success of a woman in a man's world of athletics. However, there comes a time when you say "my peace of mind is something you cannot put a price to," so after two years in this prized position, I very reluctantly left, and I got divorced. This is the second time I should have gone to counseling. Because as a professional woman my personal life was subject to scrutiny, I felt my decisions and professional judgment were being questioned—which was in reality all in my head, as the president of the institution did not want to accept my resignation. My staff and students begged me not to go, and the community leaders called every day to get me to rescind my declaration. But, with tears in my eyes, I decided to leave the area to make a fresh start at a new institution in Maryland.

The Eastern Shore of Maryland was my "Road of Damascus" experience, just like Paul's hardened heart became compassionate after encountering Jesus on his journey. My enlightening experience led to a relationship with Jesus and began the journey of self-discovery. Although it was not formal counseling, I began to frequent a local Christian bookstore. And ironically, there was not an R&B radio station signal in the entire area, so I was entertained with jazz and Gospel music. After spending two years at the Maryland institution, I received the call to return to the Conference office I'd interned with to be the public relations director and senior woman administrator.

Physically I had arrived back in Virginia, but my mind had not caught up. I was still fixated on what I thought I had lost by leaving the position of athletic director due to my divorce, and I could not see that the Conference office opportunity was a tremendous gain and far more influential. I had a fixed mindset instead of a growth mindset. My head was set looking at the past and not my future.

God has a way of getting your attention! At one point, I was trying to create materials for a board meeting with twelve college presidents, as well as planning work travel to a Title IX celebration and personal travel for my father's birthday—all while serving jury duty. Then, one day, I hit a concrete wall, figuratively and literally. I was merging onto the interstate and my car wouldn't accelerate. So I thought that the emergency brake must be on, and instead of pulling over to disable it, I tried to unlock it while driving. The company SUV I was driving skidded across four lanes and landed facing oncoming traffic beside the concrete divider. I totaled the SUV, but only had a scratch on my neck from the seat belt that protected me. Despite a lack of physical injury, I was mentally totaled, wishing I had died rather than have to face my boss, because I felt I had let him down.

This was my second car accident in six months! I was broken. I had a breakdown. I was thinking, "what is wrong with me?" I was so busy doing and not being, I just couldn't hold my head up. So my parents took me to church that Sunday. Uniquely, during devotion our church has us grouped in fives to share our prayer needs. After I shared my experience, a woman I was holding hands with said that she too had had a car accident after feeling overwhelmed and stressed at work. And that week she had started to go to counseling, and she began to feel some relief.

It was God's divine intervention. Finally, YES to therapy. It began to correct my thought processing. I became aware that I was angry at everyone that I thought had let me down, whether intentionally or unintentionally. I didn't trust and was unforgiving. I had a short fuse and couldn't take criticisms. I often traveled so I wouldn't be home alone. Specific triggers would take me back to childhood experiences where

I had no control over adult behaviors and developed harmful coping mechanisms as a result.

From my counseling sessions, I now see that I had the tendency to focus on what others thought instead of considering myself. I managed others' expectations by creating boundaries between myself and them, holding myself apart. I didn't communicate my limitations or desires to others. I didn't delegate. I didn't slow down long enough to see what I could share with others. I didn't say "no." I didn't identify myself in all the roles I served. I felt personally diminished when work didn't go well. My personal life was nonexistent.

My therapist declared that I needed to be around other women like myself. I responded, "There aren't any women around that are like me." Then I began reflecting. I may not have many peers, but I did have women coming up the ranks asking me for professional advice. So I gathered them. Now, while I support them, they are also supporting me. It is true that when you help someone else you help yourself. I began to create retreats, workshops, and gatherings that have resulted in over a dozen women of color becoming directors of athletics.

Yes, I hit a wall, but I created a door of opportunity. I created new habits, communicated my availability to others, and now consistently protect my mental intake by what I listen to and watch and what conversations I engage in. I read and did the work illustrated in self-help books such as *The Dance of*

Anger by Harriet Lerner, *The Search for Significance* by Robert McGee, and *The Four Agreements* by Don Miguel Ruiz.

These experiences have prepared me to indeed be a minister in athletics, as well as an administrator, because I can steer athletic administrators away from similar "crashes" by sharing relatable stories and guiding them to more positive and productive waters of significance. My methods focus on correcting negative self-talk and changing automatic destructive behaviors by being aware of thoughts that lead to manually controlled thoughts and actions.

Another resource I use is an assessment found within the book *Nice Girls Don't Get the Corner Office: Unconscious Mistakes Women Make That Sabotage Their Careers* by Lois P. Frankel. The assessment creates a plan of action to attack a set of self-sabotaging ways. Self-sabotage first begins in your mind and then is seen in your actions. Usually we respond on autopilot, not manual, which means we are not in conscious control of our thoughts; thus, words come tumbling out and our triggers are exposed. Athletics and higher education (to use a personal example) have many moving parts, so total control is never achieved because you have to depend on other departments and individuals for your success. As a result, frustration has a hotbed to grow in. Furthermore, being a member of an underrepresented race and gender tends to put you on the defensive instead of the offensive because you have to educate others and explain your point of view before getting the "yes." Because of this, you are always *on*.

That can put you in a place of fight or flight that you don't know how to come down from; you are on high alert all the time, which leads to depression.

Depression for the high achiever looks different than "normal" depression. The high achiever thinks that achieving more, moving up one more rung, keeping their calendar filled, taking no vacations, and being the life of the party is "success." The high achiever is a person who is too busy to feel. To them, they are chasing success by going straight up the mountain instead of spiraling up the mountain, where you can experience all four seasons, all areas of your life while you achieve. Guess what? If you go straight up the mountain, you get to the mountaintop, look down, and find that everything you love is still at the bottom. Don't chase money, chase experiences. Joy and significance should be the endgame, not happiness and success, because happiness and success requires others to be factored into the equation of your state of mind. Joy, however, is within. See, with joy, you can be stripped of your title, the mask can fall off, but you will still have talents; you will still have your influence. Then you will be significant, and that can bring you long-lasting joy. Because you impacted others' lives, when you look down the mountain you will see the people you influenced on your circular journey because you took the time to experience all of your identities. You removed the mask. You are no longer a one-dimensional person that thrives on the applause and approval of the masses, and you will be just fine "mask off." If you are like me, you will gladly take it off so you can help someone else.

Prescription for the disease to please

Identify what is motivating you or guiding your decisions. First, list the five things that most guide your decisions. This will identify what your drivers are. Are you self-driven? Many will say they are, but actually, if they dive deep, they discover how others' definition of success really drives their decisions. Do you want to be successful, or do you want to make an impact? If you wish for the top position at your organization, why? Know your reason, and you will know if you can deal with the pitfalls. Don't just want the money. Want the position for the impact you can make.

After you identify what guides your decisions, next recognize what will take you off your path; these are called your barriers. To be honest, internal obstacles will take you off your road more often than the external "isms" of the world. If you can pinpoint what you think is stopping you from reaching your destination, you can create a plan of action. Usually, it is fear and how you see the situation that is holding you back. A third party can help you know what you cannot see, especially one who has gone down the path you are traveling, one who took off the mask and now seeks significance rather than success. If you change how you see situations, you can master the uncomfortable conditions that come along with them, which is where growth and advancement occurs.

Position your mind for advancement and LeadYourShip™.

The Journey to Becoming

Tabatha L. Dandridge

As it relates to philosophy, the Oxford American College Dictionary defines the concept of *becoming* as the process of coming to be something or passing into a state. For me, that process included facing some ugly truths that I had become comfortable with, understanding past traumas and their effect on my behavior, and harnessing the boldness to confront those root causes. During one of the darkest seasons of my life, God spoke three words to me that gave me the courage, strength, and determination to come out of a destructive cycle. By those words, I was able not only to own my mistakes, but also to refuse to be governed by them any longer. Going back to the darkness, the dysfunction, and the destructive behaviors was no longer an option. The fear of being alone would lose its grip on me, and acceptance would be something I embraced from God and not from other people.

The night of my breakthrough, I was alone in my apartment feeling the sting of loneliness. The man I was involved with had not only cheated, he had also had a baby as the result of that affair. I was tired of the phone calls from other women, the disappearing at night, and the lies, but most of all the abuse. The darkness in my life at that time had engulfed me. It stuck to me like tar to a shoe. The harder I tried to make things work, the more it fell apart. I was desperate, even though I knew he didn't want anything to do with me. I had convinced myself that if I could just get him to see I was worth loving—that I was loyal, faithful, that ride or die chick—that somehow he would love me. As pathetic as it may sound, it's my truth. I was amazed at how much I could hate and love someone all at the same time. I remember thinking, I'm going to die in this situation if I don't do something to get out. In desperation I cried out to the Lord: "How did I get here?!" How did I end up in that place, where the tears from my distress had become my sustenance? Where sorrow was the air I breathed and my heart knew nothing but pain? I wanted to leave, but I didn't know how.

I had made an attempt to tell someone what was going on once over the phone, but the person on the other end of the line said, "Ugh, I have no respect for anyone who stays in an abusive situation." Needless to say, I never heard from that person again. I withdrew deeper inside myself. I didn't want to be around anyone. I was too ashamed to let anyone know I was in this position, so I hid myself out of fear of not knowing how to explain, fear of judgment, and fear of my brother ending up in jail for wanting to protect me. I cried out to God: "How?! I can't do this anymore, and if you don't bring me out of this I'm going to die here. I have nothing left; I have no fight left in me. Please help me!"

"I love you," were the words that resounded in that room. Those words penetrated my thoughts and planted roots in my soul. It was as though a lightbulb went off or a switch was turned on. For the first time I knew God loved me. It became so real to me. In that bedroom, in the safety of God's arms, He showed me times I'd given up and compromised. How fear tormented me with loneliness and thoughts of unworthiness. He shared and I listened, and in that moment something finally clicked in me. God loves me! My life would not end like this! I don't have to jump through hoops, I don't have to conform to others' image in order to be accepted, to be loved, to be wanted, because God bestowed all of that on me! I could feel His presence in that room and it washed over me like a spring shower. "You are enough," He said, "you are beautiful, you are worthy of love. You are whole in me, fearfully and wonderfully made. I love you despite you, with all your imperfections and idiosyncrasies." He never turned His back on me, despite all my mess-ups and poor decisions. His hand of grace reached down and caught me and He pulled me up to safety. It was at that moment I knew that I wanted to live. Not just exist, but live!

I found strength I didn't even know I possessed. I stopped concerning myself with the affairs of the man I was with and started focusing on the necessary steps to come all the way out of the situation. Even he realized there was something different about me. I think it scared him because he couldn't understand this new calm resolve I had, where I wasn't battling him but instead was focused. The moment I started moving toward my deliverance, things in my life started changing. I was able to get a job after being laid off for ten months; I was able to keep my jeep when I thought I would lose it. I gave notice and moved out of the apartment.

Now, it didn't end there. That was the beginning of my journey toward healing, but my road to deliverance wouldn't truly begin until much later, about a year and a half later, to be exact. I remember because it was on October 24, 2012, that my brother passed away, and I closed my shoe store on November 7 of that same year. The day I closed my store, I received a call from a coworker; she asked me to take a trip with her to Missouri and I gladly accepted. She and I were quickly forming a friendship and I appreciated her. She was the only one of my friends who showed up and offered support, and that was dear to my heart. The last two weeks had been chaotic and emotionally draining, and honestly, I just needed a break. The drive to Missouri from Virginia was long, yet we were able to share some beautiful views. The quietness of the night gave way to thought as my friend slept. I was grateful for the solitude of those stolen moments; I didn't have to put up a strong front and I could allow the tears of loss to roll down my cheeks without having to give an account for them. I always liked how soothing a drive could be. To be in new territory, well, reminded me of my brother. He was the real adventurer in the family. The one thing about him I loved the most was his tenaciousness. When he set his mind to doing something, he did it! I so admired that quality.

As we drove into St. Louis, I was in awe of the Arch. It was just as magnificent as it was the first time I saw it. Two more hours, my friend said. I thought to myself, two more hours, man this is a long drive. Fifteen hours to be exact. As we drove into the town of St. Roberts, I remember thinking . . . I could live here. Little did I know, six months later I would be calling it my home. It was in St. Roberts that I would find fellowship with a women's ministry, and, while on a women's retreat, in the final service I would come face to face with the root of the issue that caused so much chaos in my life.

As I sat there in the service, we were asked to think about our life, our struggles, any reoccurring patterns of dysfunction, and our behaviors. Then, we were to ask God to show us the root of that behavior, struggle, or pattern, because what we were seeing was the symptoms of something deeper. As I sat there, thinking over my life and what had ultimately set me on the road to wholeness, I came to the revelation that my issues were relational. I prayed, "So God, why do I struggle with feelings of inadequacy and belonging? I'm all too familiar with the symptoms. I know I've asked before, but this time I am ready to see it. With you, I am ready to face it." The room seemed to go quiet, and for a while it was as though I were the only one there. As afraid as I was of what He'd reveal, I was determined to get to the root of my feelings. It wasn't that long ago that God had delivered me from that abusive situation, and I knew I didn't ever want to go back to that behavior that had gotten me there in the first place. My childhood came to mind. It was then that I'd first started feeling alone, dejected, and unaccepted.

Growing up, I felt like an outsider in my family. As a child, as early as nine or ten years old, I can remember feeling like the outcast. I didn't appear to be much like my mom, dad, or siblings. They are beautifully social and easygoing people who can make friends wherever they go. I was socially awkward, shy, and introverted. Although I knew and still know my family loves me, I can remember feeling like the black sheep; I never seemed to fit in. I also remember feeling left out by my extended family. That fed my psyche and perpetuated the feelings of non-acceptance. It sounds convoluted, I know, yet those feelings of inferiority were strongest around certain people whose comments and candor when I was a child changed how I perceived things. Everything seemed to play on those emotions.

I can recall a time as a young adult when my sister and I were talking after a visit from my aunts. My sister had just gotten off the phone with one of our cousins, who had been there when our aunts visited. During that conversation, my cousin had inquired as to why they acted funny toward me. My sister had asked, "What do you mean?"

My cousin had responded, "Why don't they talk to Tammy?"—my childhood nickname—"Why do they leave her out of things? They treat her different."

As my sister related this conversation to me, for a moment I was quiet; I'd been saying that for years. I wanted to cry, but as the tears started to fill my eyes, I started having this overwhelming sense of release. For the first time someone else had noticed what I'd been saying all along. At that moment it was no longer "just my imagination." It was validated. I could have gotten salty over why it took my cousin saying something before anyone would believe it, but honestly I didn't care. It was exposed. My sister made a point of talking to my aunt, one in particular; she apologized, stating it was never her intention, and that she would make a point of including me and talking to me more. She did, but honestly my heart had grown so callused as a way of protecting myself that it didn't matter much to me anymore—at least that's the lie I told myself—and through half-hearted acceptance on my part I just moved on.

I thought of all of this at that women's retreat. As I sat there in that conference room, taking everything in, I noted that God called what I'd experienced rejection. According to the Biblical Counseling Database, "rejection occurs when a person or group of people excludes an individual and refuses to acknowledge or accept them" (http://biblicalcounselingdatabase.net/rejection-and-abandonment). God was showing me in that moment that the spirit of rejection had attached itself to me early on. It came with subtle words like "you don't look like your mom or dad." It tagged along with the jokes about who my daddy was. It happened through not being included on phone calls or requested to come visit. All of this fed my insecurities and damaged my sense of belonging.

God was showing me the seed, the root of my inner turmoil. The searching, the wanting to belong, to be wanted, to feel loved, all stemmed from rejection. Each experience, no matter how small, built upon each other until rejection became a full-fledged stronghold in my life. My emotions were being manipulated by a force I didn't recognize or know existed. All I knew was that it hurt and I'd felt alone. It isolated me, eventually causing me to seek acceptance from people who were never meant to solidify wholeness for me.

Let me tell you, I spent years looking for validation in the arms of people just as broken as me. Each failed relationship, friendship, and marriage took its toll, ripping away pieces of me, causing my life to leak out through holes of low self-esteem, no self-worth, and no sense of value.

I realized: how could others love me when I didn't love me? I wanted people to see something in me, yet I saw less and less in me. How could anyone tell me I was valuable or worth having, when after each failure I couldn't see any worth or value?

With the root exposed, I now had the responsibility, with God's help, of putting in the work to become whole. I had to be intentional about not running to that familiar place when I felt lonely, not rehearsing negative words spoken to me, and not seeing myself as less than.

For some of you, your breakthrough may come from peeling back the layers like an artichoke until you get to the heart of the matter. For others, it may come instantaneously because you have the strength to face the force at the root. Understand that no one is responsible for your happiness but you. Stop trying to find your self-worth in other people! Stop trying to change people to fit your picture of what a happy life is, and stop conforming to the image of what someone else's definition of happy looks like. You are responsible for you! When you're broken, you attract brokenness, and despite what they say, two halves don't make a whole. You have to come to a place of wholeness on your own and allow others to enter into that happiness. Those who pose a threat to your peace need to be kicked out immediately.

Listen, my story is not about the person or persons who played roles in my dysfunction, but rather what caused me to allow the behavior. I don't negate the fact that horrible things happened at the hands of others, but ultimately, my brokenness and skewed perception of myself caused me to stay in situations I knew in my core were detrimental to my health, growth, purpose, and wellbeing. I learned to never be afraid to be alone. God will hold your hand and walk you through the lowest valley one step at a time until you look up and notice you are on the other side of defeat.

Prescription for reoccurring rejection

Start now. What one thing can you do to change your life for the better? What's keeping you back from realizing your biggest dream? Get a journal and go someplace quiet. Ask the difficult questions and write what you see. Read it aloud, then ask God for the plan and strategy to get there.

Finding My Voice

Sabrina Thomas

There is nothing worse than living an unfulfilled life. If there is one lesson I have learned these past years, it is to not allow my fears to prevent me from pursuing my dreams and being what God has destined me to be.

My name is Sabrina Thomas. I'm a mother of two beautiful boys and a special needs advocate. I'm also a passionate advocate for autism and special education. I have dedicated my life to providing resources and tools for special needs families. My passion for autism awareness was inspired by my son Omar, who has autism and cerebral palsy, as well as an intellectual disability.

Like everybody else, I've always had dreams. At one point in my life, I wanted to be a nurse, but all that changed when I gave birth to a special needs child. My whole life became focused on taking care of my special needs son, knowing that I was all he had. I've had to care for my special needs son's every need while fighting against an unjust system that did not seem to care. Little did I know that all that was preparing me for something greater. I never thought I'd be anything other than a mom to a special needs kid; being a business owner never even crossed my mind. However, today, I'm an advocate, a speaker, a coach, and an author. This is the story of how I started to find my voice.

I spent so many years advocating for my son and helping others without fully realizing what I could achieve for myself. I never thought I had what it takes. But I realized that I didn't want to live without fully experiencing life. I wanted to live a fulfilled life. I didn't want to just exist. So, I prayed and I asked God for directions, and He gave me all the confidence I needed to go after what I wanted. I realized that it has always been in me. I just needed to dig a little deeper to become what I was destined to be.

I'm not going to pretend that it was easy by any stretch of the imagination. In fact, I cannot count the number of times that I tried to give up. I was crippled by my fear of failure, my fear of what people would think. But I decided to go for it. I put all my fears behind me and put everything I had into chasing my dreams, and I've never being happier!

So I made up my mind to start going to conferences, to surround myself with confident women, women who knew what they wanted in life and were not afraid to go after it. This is probably one of the best decisions I ever made. It had such a positive impact on my life. It has afforded me the opportunity to become a businesswoman and not just to work a nine to five job. It was also one of the hardest things I had ever done. The odds were not in my favor, as when I started, I had two adult sons, one of them with special needs. I didn't think I could pull it off until I did!

Being a mother is one of my biggest joys that has also given me one of my toughest challenges. I had dreams and things I wanted to achieve, but I was too scared to go after them because I did not want to neglect my kids. The guilt always managed to rope me in each time I tried to step out of my comfort zone and achieve something great. But after a while, I decided to just go for it, knowing my kids would be happier with a mother who is fulfilled. When I look back at my days of struggling, I'm completely amazed at all the things I've been able to achieve in such a short period of time. Things I probably wouldn't have achieved if I had allowed my fear to cripple me. I'm so glad I was brave enough to take that first step.

It took me years of relentless trying and sleepless nights to figure it out. There are so many other women out there who are still struggling to improve their conditions. So how was I able to achieve it? What did I do differently?

The first thing you must understand is that the battle is first won in the mind. Our mind is such a powerful tool, and we don't even know how powerful it is. Another step to finding your voice is believing in yourself. I cannot stress this enough. If you don't believe in yourself, there is really no point in trying. For me, the moment I realized that I could do it was the moment I liberated myself from the fear of failure and started living fully. I stopped feeling sorry for myself and realized that everything I had been through before that point was only preparing me for this moment. You must learn to find joy in every circumstance you find yourself in. You need to train your mind to believe that you can overcome every obstacle in your path. I erroneously assumed that taking care of my special needs kid would consume all my time and prevent me from going after my dreams. It turns out that it was preparing me for greater things.

My twenty-plus years in the hospitality field and the eighteen years I spent taking care of my special needs son and advocating for him were what eventually gave me the foundation for my career. The most rewarding part of my career comes from being able to give parents, families, and caregivers the power and knowledge they need, and to be the best possible advocate for those with special needs. I wouldn't have this knowledge if I had not spent all those years taking care of my son. I know firsthand how overwhelming life can be when you have a child with special needs, which is why I find so much joy in speaking about what I've learned and sharing my life with others. My goal is that my messages will be inclusive, transparent, and encouraging.

Another thing I've learned on this journey is the importance of forgiveness. This may seem like a trivial issue, but it really isn't. You must learn to forgive those who hurt you to find the peace you need to become what you're destined to be. It is only when you're truly at peace with yourself and your world that you can do the things God has destined you to do. It might not be easy, but it is worth it. It shows your strength of character—which is something you'll need to succeed as an entrepreneur.

My ability to maintain a positive attitude has also helped a great deal. Imagine the audacity of thinking you can change the course of your life while approaching fifty years of age. Imagine thinking you can change your narrative at this stage in your life, yet I dared to do all that. Despite the little doubts and worries, I never allowed the negativity to weigh me down. I had to change my mindset. I decided to channel a lot of positivity into my life and to look at the negatives as positives. I did not know that the time I spent volunteering and advocating for others was simply preparing me for my purpose in life. I was becoming, and I didn't even realize it.

I also learned to work on myself. I discovered that when you begin to exploit your abilities and potential, you'll be amazed at how much depth there is to you. Till this day, I'm pleasantly surprised at how much I'm able to achieve. I have come to realize that I am a goldmine. All I needed to succeed was in me, and all I had to do was dig a little deeper. You hold the power to succeed in your hands if only you begin to realize that no one can do it for you, and that you're the only person that can unearth all that potential. So what is stopping you?

I did not realize how much I was capable of until I started taking certain critical steps. I'm a coach today, but I didn't just start coaching. This is something I have always done. I would give advice to special needs families around me, and I didn't even know the effect of all that until I became an entrepreneur. I didn't realize that I was finding my voice.

I learned to market my skills. As much as I love to give back, I realized that I could also make a career out of this. Learning the value of my intellectual property was a real eye opener! Now I can make money from doing what I love, and I get to give back on a wider scale. Everything changed as soon as I started thinking like an entrepreneur. I saw everything in a new light, and I began to see possibilities where I never would have thought possible. I am much more informed and enlightened than I was a few years ago, and with information comes power. Even with my children, I can now provide better care for them, and all this wouldn't have been possible if I hadn't decided to break free of the prison of fear that I had created for myself. Fear of failure, of the unknown, has killed so many ideas before they even took off. I refused to become another statistic for people who thought but were never able to actualize their ideas. I took charge of my life and I have not looked back since.

I have achieved so much in two years. Things I never thought I'd achieve. I am a speaker, an advocate, a writer, and a certified IEP coach. Imagine if I had allowed my fear to control me. I wouldn't have achieved any of these things. That is not to say it was easy. There were nights after I transitioned from my full-time job to my part-time job when I woke up in a panic thinking about the weight of my decision. I worried about everything. I worried about my sons, especially Omar. I worried about my ability to provide for them, about who would care for them while I was away trying to make things work. But in all this, one thing I realized is that if there is a will, there is a way. If you want something bad enough, you will find a way to make it happen. Looking back at things, I'm amazed at how I was able to overcome some of those hurdles. There were times when I had to attend meetings and couldn't find someone to look after my son when I said to myself, "is this really worth it?" But somehow, I found the will to forge ahead, to persist despite what seemed like insurmountable hurdles. Life is not a bed of roses, but it is in those difficult moments when it seems all hope is lost that you realize how resilient you really are. I had to dig deep, to be creative, and somehow, I was almost always able to come up with a solution.

Prescription for the inflammation of feeling scared to fail

You must learn to be decisive. If you make up your mind about something, follow through. It is okay to have doubts, but learn to trust your intuition. There were so many times when it felt like I was making the biggest mistake of my life. However, with time, I have learned to trust my intuition, and it has never failed me.

I would be lying if I said I don't get scared, but I am no longer scared of moving forward. I have experienced so many changes in such a short time and have learned so many lessons while at it. My biggest takeaway from all this is that it is never too late to learn or start anew. Never allow fear of failure or fear of what people will say stop you from going after your dreams. You're stronger than you know; all you need to do is dig a little deeper. It is never too late to become who you are meant to be.

I thought my son's cerebral palsy and autism diagnosis was the end of my dreams; turns out it was the foundation for my becoming . . .

The Truth of the Matter Is...

Gwendolyn Winston-Marrow

When you've lived as long as I have, you have had many pivotal moments in your life, so deciding which one to write about wasn't an easy task. Out of them all—the molestation, the rape, the rejection, and all the false accusations—I kept coming back to this one pivotal moment that left me feeling so abandoned.

It was June 2006, and I was in Texas at a hospital visiting my cousin, who was both a daughter and friend to me. She had been battling colon cancer for over two years, and the doctors had said there was nothing more they could do except make her comfortable. She had decided she didn't want to stay in the hospital; she wanted to go home. During the drive back, she talked about her and her family's move to Virginia. She was so excited about going to Virginia because she wanted to talk to the doctors there about her treatment. The movers had packed up everything in the house and they were supposed to be on their way to their new place in Staunton, Virginia, but the doctors had said she was too sick to travel. Instead, we were being told to go home and make "arrangements." We had to prepare for something we hadn't expected, especially at that point in her life. She had been doing so well, and she and her husband were in the process of adopting a little girl. Having seen how well she was doing since it had all started over two years ago, I refused to believe the doctors. I continued to pray and believe for her complete healing so she wouldn't have to go through it anymore. She was too young to die, and besides, she had two young children, ages three and five, to raise; surely she was not going to die, regardless of what the doctors said.

Watching her get worse day by day was so hard, but I knew that things could get better because they had before, back when she was first diagnosed. I remember when she called me to give me the news that she had been to the doctor and had to go back for her diagnosis; she was so afraid. I told her not to worry, that I would be there. I talked to my husband and to my pastor, who was also my boss at the time, and told them I had to go. When I got there I was shocked to see how much weight she had lost. We went to the doctor the next day, and that is when she was given her diagnosis, stage 4 colon cancer, and that she only had maybe two months to live. Being with her while she went through the chemotherapy treatment and seeing the affect it was having on her was hard, but also so necessary. Sometimes all I could do was hold her in my arms and rock her until the pain went away.

We had to drive two hours to the hospital in San Antonio for her to get her chemo treatments. Her baby boy would get sick every time we went. She said it was motion sickness, but I believe he was emotionally and physically responding to what his mother was going through.

After that initial diagnosis, I stayed with her for over two months until she was stronger, able to eat again and beginning to gain her weight back. At that point, she told me it was okay for me to go back home. I really hadn't wanted to leave her, but she had insisted that she was going to be fine, so I reluctantly headed back home. She really was doing fine. She planned a family reunion in July 2005 and we all went back to Texas and celebrated with them. We had a wonderful time. In December 2005, they came to Virginia for Christmas and then left to go to Indiana to visit her husband's family for the New Year. Everything appeared to be going great for her.

When her husband called me in 2006 to tell me she was unable to travel because she had gotten sick again and they had put her in the hospital, I couldn't believe it. She had been fine six months ago, so surely she could not be going through this again. He called her sisters and told them that if they wanted to see her before she passed, they needed to get there as soon as possible. Her sisters arrived and we continued to try to keep things as normal as possible for her and the kids. Even though things didn't look good, I refused to be moved by what I was seeing. The hospice nurse came twice a week to check on us. She would say it wasn't going to be long now, and ask if we had made any arrangements. I continued to pray and believe she was going to be all right because I didn't want to believe what the nurse was saying. However, on Thursday, June 15, 2006, she lost her battle to cancer.

The hospice nurse stayed with us until they came to pick up her body. We sent the kids to stay with a neighbor until they left. Numb and in disbelief, I watched everything that happened, feeling as though it wasn't happening. Then, when they finally got there, as they were taking her out of the house, a wind began to blow and the wind chimes at the front entrance of the house began to make the most beautiful sound. I knew then that she was at peace. But how was I to feel about my prayer request for her healing? That was not how I expected her to be healed. Instead, we had to move forward with the preparations for her move to Virginia in a whole different way, with her body being shipped to Virginia for a funeral.

Her husband and sister made all the funeral arrangements as I prepared to go home. Once I was back in Virginia, there was no time to grieve; I had too much to do, as my mom was having bypass surgery Tuesday, June 20. We had to believe everything was going to go well for her. The next day, I went back to the hospital to see how my mother was doing after her surgery. The doctor said the surgery went well and that she was doing fine. Mom was in a good mood and was excited about the good report. She had visitors and they were all laughing and talking. Relieved, I went off to help my cousin's family, to get clothes for the kids to wear to their mother's funeral that Saturday. All their things were still packed and with the movers. Having gotten their clothes, I headed to Ashland to take them to their dad. My husband and son were with me because we were going to the hospital to see my mom after I dropped the kids' clothes off. Then I got a phone call from the hospital saying that I needed to come to the hospital right away because my mother's doctor wanted to talk to us.

I said, "Okay," turned around, and headed to the hospital. I really wasn't concerned because I had been to the hospital earlier during the day and she was doing fine.

We got to the hospital waiting room and the doctor asked, "Is this all of the immediate family?" After we said it was, the doctor said, "We did all we could but we couldn't save her."

WHAT?! We were stunned. She was fine. They had said the surgery went well. What happened?

When we asked, the doctor said, "We're not sure. We have to run more tests."

I was still numb from my cousin's death, I had just gone to see my mom, who was just fine a few hours ago, and now she was dead. I couldn't make any sense of any of it. Exactly one week after my cousin's death on Thursday, June 15, 2006, my mother died, on Thursday, June 22, 2006. I wondered, What's wrong with me? What is wrong with my faith? Why are my prayers not being answered? What is wrong with my relationship with God?

I felt there was no time to grieve, no time to spend trying to figure it out; I had to stay strong for everyone else. There was no time to deal with my emotions; I had to push those feelings back and keep on going. I had to attend my cousin's funeral that weekend, minister on Sunday, and make arrangements for my mother's funeral. My sister called me and told me we had an appointment at the funeral home on Sunday at 2:00 p.m. I told her, "Okay, I'll be there."

That Sunday, I had gone to McKenny, Virginia, to minister and was on my way to Ashland for the 2:00 p.m. appointment when I got a call from my sister saying they were going to the funeral home just then, at 12:45 p.m. I said, "Okay, but I had to minister in McKenny this morning and I'm over an hour away, so I won't be able to get there. I thought the appointment was at 2:00 p.m.?"

She replied, "Yeah, but we're in Ashland already so we are going now."

I said, "Okay, let me know if you need me to do anything." I went home and sat down with all these thoughts going through my mind but refusing to feel anything. Just going through the motions and continuing to say "I'm fine" whenever asked how I was and if I needed anything. I didn't know what else to say. I didn't want to feel anything. All I could think was, I've always tried to be there for others, so why do

I feel so alone, so abandoned, so rejected as I go through all of this? Why are there no people calling or visiting? I thought that's what people did in times like these.

Ever been afraid to feel because the emotional pain is so deep that you are afraid if you go there, you won't come back? Well, after the two funerals were over, that's where I was, all alone with my thoughts. I was keeping my cousin's kids while their dad found a place for them to stay, and at the same time getting things ready for my son to go away to college. I had too much to do to feel anything, so I just kept going through the motions of everyday life: work, children, husband, and still holding on to the pain.

I had spent over thirteen years taking on the responsibility of being god in my life. Regarding my cousin's and mother's death, I had the mindset that because it wasn't done the way I thought it should be, there had to be something wrong with me, my prayer life, and my relationship with God. Because of that mindset, I stopped praying like I used to. I prayed, but with no real expectation. I second-guessed everything I did. In all that time, I didn't stop to think about the fact that when they told my cousin she only had two months to live, she lived over two years longer than what the doctors had said. My prayer was answered, but I was so busy wanting more that I wasn't thankful for what she had been given. I also forgot that my mom often told me she was tired, and that maybe what happened was an answer to her prayer. I allowed that whole situation to impact how I saw myself and how I saw my God. I put myself in the prison of inadequacy with my stinking thinking.

I have had to confront myself about all my excuses for not "removing the face." I have come to realize that if I deal with myself and make myself the focus of my transition, then I can no longer blame someone else for where I am. As long as I blamed someone else for my circumstances, I didn't have to do the work of dealing with me. I believe that the face of pride—insisting that I'm fine, I got this, I'm okay, I don't need anything, I'm good—is one of the hardest faces for people to realize they wear.

Sometime long after the funerals, I asked my pastor, "Why didn't anyone from the church come to see me or call me?"

He said, "We thought you were okay." I wonder how they got that idea. Could it have possibly been from me?

Because I wanted the image of having it all together and not needing anyone, it cost me more than I realized. It cost me friends, finances, relationships, and destiny. So the first face I had to remove was the face of pride, of "I'm fine . . ." I had to remove that face first so that I could reveal the other faces behind it: fear, abandonment, shame, rejection, loneliness, inadequacy, anger, unbelief, unworthiness, and unforgiveness. I have been my own worst enemy.

Prescription for the phantom pain of pride

These are some questions I had to ask myself during this process of confronting myself so that I could begin removing the face and dealing with the pain:

1. What was I saying to myself about myself? I had to take responsibility for my thought life.

2. How did I really see myself; as a grasshopper or an eagle? Would I just keep hopping around in the low places of my life, or would I take on the responsibility of moving forward and soaring? My mindset made a difference.

3. Who and what did I need to confront? Because by not confronting the issue and/or the person, I gave the issue permission to stay and the person permission to continue to treat me the way he or she did.

Now I am doing the work that I should have done years ago, moment by moment and day by day. It's amazing to see my prayers being answered; it's not always the way I want, but it's the way that is best for me. So as you remove the face, be honest with yourself and live an authentic life. You will find and come to love the real you that has been hiding for so long. As my coach always says, "You just have to DO THE WORK." Remember, it's a process, and it's not easy, but it is so necessary and so rewarding.

#YESCHANGE!!!

NOW WHAT?

Today is the commencement day for your journey through the pages of this anthology. A commencement is not the end of something; it's a celebration of your progress and accomplishments coupled with a healthy dose of inspiration and encouragement for your future endeavors. It's the beginning of what's next. Much like a graduation, I am sure you have had moments of reflection as you peered into the lives of these writers who have journeyed with you, cheering you on in your process. You've taken mental snapshots to capture the moments where you felt relief or comfort or were able to address what you repressed for so long.

Consider this your commencement speech: Every writer in this anthology has challenged you with an action to aid you in your healing process to wholeness. Though this anthology is ending, your personal anthology of hope and healing is just beginning. God is writing your life's next chapter on your heart, and it looks NOTHING like what you have experienced in the past. We all know the pain of "faces," and we have shared our journey with you. Your charge? Don't use this book as a memoir; use it instead as an impetus for change. Your trigger points are now turning points . . . Don't stop at pain; get to purpose!

Once you have done the work, you OWE it to yourself to move forward. This is NOT the end. As you dig beneath the surface and continue to uncover the things that have disguised your true identity and have held you back from your God-given purpose, remember that His desire is to bring you into new places, new memories, new references, new relationships, and a new normal.

Practice the remedies shared in this book. Listen to the directions written deep within your soul . . . But most importantly, remove the face, turn your tassel, and live!

Signed,
Silent Contributor to Your Change

About the Authors

Ifedayo Greenway is a licensed minister, bestselling author, and personal development coach who works to impact and change lives by helping women embark on their change journey. She is passionate about her faith and her assignment as a mother to nurture the lives of her three children. She is the CEO of IG & M.O.R.E. (Ife Greenway and Ministry of Real Empowerment) and uses her personal journey to strengthen others. Her "call to coaching" led her to start the Movement of Becoming (MOB) where she empowers women to become more. Her goal is to help women learn to leverage their place of pain as a pathway and as momentum for forward movement. Ifedayo is also the event producer of Changing Faces, an empowering makeover movement that encourages women to see themselves through the eyes of purpose instead of circumstance.

Learn more at www.igandmore.com

ABOUT THE AUTHORS

Shakita Wilson is the founder and visionary of The RUTH Foundation (Redeemed Under The Holy Spirit), a nonprofit organization geared toward individuals who have faced challenges with the criminal justice system and are seeking another chance. She is a mother, servant, and facilitator, and is passionate about impacting and changing lives.

With a degree in paralegal law and over fifteen years of investigative skills, she uses the same skill sets in her personal, spiritual, and professional life. In addition to being a published writer, she was recognized by the Community Foundation for the "Power of Good" for her service in the community. Shakita is committed to transparency and being relatable, using her personal journey and experiences to give others hope in hopeless situations. Shakita encourages others to find their true purpose in life while pursuing their passion.

Contact Shakita at shakitarenee@gmail.com

Kiara Washington is a native of Richmond, Virginia, where she was raised by her mother along with her three other siblings. Growing up, Kiara was drawn to the arts, having an affinity toward music, modeling, and singing. However, her inner voice told her a time would come when her life required more from her.

That time would come sooner than anyone expected. At the age of twenty-seven, Kiara's life changed forever. On December 11, 2017, she witnessed her mother pass away from stage four cancer. This was truly the most life-altering experience she has endured. It left her with many difficult choices to make.

Forever mindful of the lessons from her mother's life, she has chosen to not be broken. She has chosen to use her mother's transition as her major motivation. She has decided to heal the family's bloodline by starting with herself.

Learn more at www.kiarawashingtonspeaks.com

ABOUT THE AUTHORS

Lynnetta M. Seabury is a well-rounded mentor and educator. Her mission in life is to create environments where individuals discover, then walk in, their destiny. She holds a baccalaureate degree in business management and a master's degree in management. Lynnetta is currently the head of the science department at a private school, with a career spanning over twenty years as an educator. Lynnetta was honored to be the keynote speaker at her college graduation.

Lynnetta's unique style has earned her respect as an effective leader, empowering many to walk in confidence of who they are. She has also helped organizations improve processes and productivity. Lynnetta has a powerful outreach to millennials, building strong mentee/mentor relationships throughout the United States. Lynnetta is happily married to Jeffrey Seabury and is the proud mom of two handsome young kings, David and Jonathan.

Contact Lynnetta at asklynne25@gmail.com

Sandra L. Parker is the CEO of Speak Life on Purpose, LLC, a movement created to inspire, motivate, and encourage women to speak words of life, no matter where they find themselves in life. She is a teacher, speaker, and facilitator that loves to encourage women to be bold and authentic. She is also a licensed minister who depends heavily on her faith in every area of her life.

As a subject matter expert in finding purpose after pain, she shares her personal journey to help women embrace change and access their personal power in order to grow. She is passionate about seeing women turn their pain into positive growth. She believes that without pain there is no progress. She is supported in her endeavors by her lovely daughter, Natasha.

Contact Sandra at speaklifeonpurposellc@gmail.com

ABOUT THE AUTHORS

Felicia Ellis, affectionately known as Fee, is a trained therapist and the founder of HerHealing, who desires to help women find healing, hope, and happiness. What began as a God-given revelation she has evolved into a community of empowerment and a network of healing. Felicia realized that there is an urgent need for internal healing among women who have gone through trying times or traumatic events. Felicia also recognized that many women hurt in silence due to a lack of consistent support and understanding from those closest to them. Her vision is to pair women around the globe based on their shared experiences by providing a variety of ways to connect through her website.

According to Fee, "I believe there is strength in numbers, and when surrounded by the genuine support of friends, family, or strangers—healing occurs."

Learn more at www.HerHealingConnection.com

Charleta D. M. Harvey, MAML, is a native Washingtonian, having been born and raised in the nation's capital. Her personal motto is that "it takes us all to lift us all." She is a military spouse, proud mom of two, and entrepreneur. She holds a master's degree in business with an emphasis on management and leadership. Professionally, she has been coaching and consulting since 2004, most recently specializing in the use of people analytics for the delivery of organizational learning and development training resources. Charleta has served in a variety of capacities, including a stint on the Corporate Advisory Panel of the United Services Automobile Association (USAA), as well as a community partner of the H.E.R. Shelter of Portsmouth, Virginia. She is passionate about youth empowerment and entrepreneurialism, as well as issues that impact women's wellness.

Contact Charleta at Charleta@design-your-thoughts.com

ABOUT THE AUTHORS

Laura C. Bembry has over fifteen years of experience working within the information technology field but has a passion for the growth and development of others. This passion led her to obtain her bachelor's degree in psychology and a master's degree within human resource management. Her mission is to uplift and encourage others who may be faced with similar challenges by sharing transparent and insightful experiences that will add to their lives. Laura is the recipient of the 2019 Outstanding Leader Award for the Mount Western Branch in Chesapeake, Virginia.

Learn more at www.linkedin.com/in/op2miss

Jackie Togun is a native of Richmond, Virginia. She is the oldest of ten children, mother of four, grandmother of nine, and great-grandmother of five. She was licensed to preach the Gospel in May 1995, and later ordained. Her academic pursuits include a bachelor of general studies in education and business management from Virginia Commonwealth University, Richmond, Virginia, and a master of arts in education from Oral Roberts University, Tulsa, Oklahoma. She has worked as an educator for over two decades. She has been connected to ministries within the church that include nursery, hospitality, music, children's church, intercessory prayer, women's ministry, single's ministry, Christian education, and elders council. Some of the community outreach programs in which she has served or is currently serving include Bible study for seniors, prison ministry, street ministry, and enhancement programs for women, which teach things like self-love, self-empowerment, and self-engagement.

Contact Jackie at jacquelinetogun@yahoo.com

ABOUT THE AUTHORS

Monique A. J. Smith, a sports management veteran of thirty years, is a leadership strategist for both athletic departments and individuals who wish to advance in athletics/sports. Her business, Seeds of Empowerment®, was named one of fifty businesses to watch by the BOSS Network. Smith is a Hampton University adjunct teaching sports management courses. As the host of the nationally recognized weekly podcast *A Chat in the Garden with Monique A. J. Smith, Where Significance Blooms in Athletics & Sports*, she spotlights women of color in athletics/sports to her 1.5k followers.

Smith is a native of Waverly, Virginia. She is married to Thomas Smith of Newport News, Virginia, whom she met in college. She calls him "The Blessing" because their union is a testament of what God's faithfulness will provide; he is a loving and supportive partner of eight years.

Learn more at http://MoniqueAJSmith.as.me

Tabatha L. Dandridge provides insight and information—filled with hope and inspiration—about moving forward in purpose and power. She is an ordained minister, blogger, event producer, businesswoman, and speaker. Tabatha has been involved in ministry for over three years. Equipped with her knowledge and experience, she helps people to understand the power force they are through using the word of God. Tabatha's mantra is that you don't have to be governed by past behaviors; you can make your mistakes into the stepping stones to your next level. Tabatha's passion is to empower through insightful and thought-provoking teaching, workshops, seminars, and events.

Learn more at www.PoweredForChange.com

ABOUT THE AUTHORS

Sabrina Thomas is a passionate autism and special education advocate and special needs empowerment coach who provides resources and tools to assist special needs families. The mother of two beautiful sons, one of whom has special needs, Sabrina believes that by raising awareness, we will enhance the lives of people with special needs now and in the future.

Sabrina's innate compassion and enthusiasm, combined with her love for her son and her appreciation for all people living with special needs, are the driving force behind her awareness initiatives. Rooted in her beliefs of giving back and effective advocacy, Sabrina is a supporter of and regular volunteer for organizations that support autism and other developmental disabilities.

As an author, speaker, and advocate, shining a light on the joys and challenges of parenting children with special needs, Sabrina's mission is to ensure special needs families never go at it alone and always feel supported.

Learn more at www.sabrinatspeaks.com

Gwendolyn Winston-Marrow is the innovator for Gwen's Inspirational Moments, a platform that she uses to inspire and encourage others to keep moving forward. She has been married for over forty years. She is a mother and grandmother, as well as a powerful orator and workshop facilitator. For over twenty-five years, Gwen has been facilitating powerful life-changing workshops that exhort, encourage, and empower others to be the motivational force that transforms their lives.

She attended Virginia State University, Virginia Commonwealth University, and Fredericksburg Bible College. She was employed by the Department of Social Services and is a former Army reservist.

She is compassionate about restoration and healing in peoples' lives and uses the limpidity of her own life to prove that your place of pain can also become your place of power.

Contact Gwendolyn at gwm.movingforward@gmail.com

CREATING DISTINCTIVE BOOKS
WITH INTENTIONAL RESULTS

We're a collaborative group of creative masterminds with a mission to produce high-quality books to position you for monumental success in the marketplace.

Our professional team of writers, editors, designers, and marketing strategists work closely together to ensure that every detail of your book is a clear representation of the message in your writing.

Want to know more?
Write to us at info@publishyourgift.com
or call (888) 949-6228

Discover great books, exclusive offers, and more at
www.PublishYourGift.com

Connect with us on social media

@publishyourgift

www.ingramcontent.com/pod-product-compliance
Lightning Source LLC
Chambersburg PA
CBHW052047070526
44584CB00017B/2086